# Four Dichotomies in Spanish

Examining four dichotomies in Spanish, this book shows how to reduce the six to ten rules common in textbooks for each contrast to a single binary distinction. That distinction is a form of totality vs. part, easier to see in some of the dichotomies, but present in all of them.

Every chapter is example-driven, and many of those examples come from writing by students. Readers can test out for themselves the explanation at work in the examples provided. Then, those examples are explained step by step. In addition to examples from writing by college students, there are examples from RAE (Real Academia Española), from scholars, from writers, from Corpes XXI (RAE), from the Centro Virtual Cervantes, and from the Internet. Many of those examples are presented to the reader as exercises, and answers are provided.

This book was written for teachers of Spanish as a second language (L2) and for minors or majors of Spanish as an L2. It will also benefit teachers and learners of other L2s with some of these dichotomies.

**Luis H. González** is an associate professor of Spanish and linguistics at Wake Forest University. He completed his Ph.D. at the University of California, Davis. His main areas of research are semantic roles, case, reflexivization, clitic doubling, differential object marking, dichotomies in language, Spanish linguistics, and second language learning. He is the co-author of *Gramática para la composición* (Georgetown UP), a Spanish advanced grammar and writing textbook, now in its third edition (2016). He is also the author of *Cómo entender y cómo enseñar* por *y* para, published by Routledge in 2020.

D1378017

# Four Dichotomies in Spanish
## Adjective Position, Adjectival Clauses, Ser/Estar, and Preterite/Imperfect

**Luis H. González**

Spanish List Advisor:
**Javier Muñoz-Basols**

Routledge
Taylor & Francis Group

LONDON AND NEW YORK

First published 2021
by Routledge
2 Park Square, Milton Park, Abingdon, Oxon OX14 4RN

and by Routledge
52 Vanderbilt Avenue, New York, NY 10017

*Routledge is an imprint of the Taylor & Francis Group, an informa business*

©2021 Luis H. González; Chapter 3, Luis H. González and Michael Davern;
Chapter 4, Luis H. González and Peter Till

The right of Luis H. González to be identified as author of this work has
been asserted by him in accordance with sections 77 and 78 of the Copyright,
Designs and Patents Act 1988.

*British Library Cataloguing-in-Publication Data*
A catalogue record for this book is available from the British Library

*Library of Congress Cataloging-in-Publication Data*
Names: González, Luis H., author.
Title: Four dichotomies in Spanish : adjective position, adjectival clauses,
ser/estar, and preterite/imperfect / Luis H. González.
Description: London ; New York : Routledge, 2020. | Includes bibliographical
references and index.
Identifiers: LCCN 2020031523 (print) | LCCN 2020031524 (ebook) |
ISBN 9780367517281 (hardback) | ISBN 9781003054962 (ebook)
Subjects: LCSH: Spanish language--Adjective. | Spanish language--Study and
teaching--Foreign speakers.
Classification: LCC PC4241 .G66 2020 (print) | LCC PC4241 (ebook) |
DDC 468.2/421--dc23
LC record available at https://lccn.loc.gov/2020031523
LC ebook record available at https://lccn.loc.gov/2020031524

ISBN: 978-0-367-51728-1 (hbk)
ISBN: 978-1-003-05496-2 (ebk)

Typeset in Times New Roman
by Deanta Global Publishing Services, Chennai, India

To those who realize that school is more about learning than about teaching.

# Contents

## 2   Whole/part matters: Nonrestrictive and restrictive adjectival (relative) clauses     42

LUIS H. GONZÁLEZ

## 3   *Estar* expresses change of state; most learners already have *ser* in their native language     70

LUIS H. GONZÁLEZ AND MICHAEL DAVERN

**4 The preterite is like entering or leaving a room; the
imperfect is like staying in it** 87

LUIS H. GONZÁLEZ AND PETER TILL

# Tables

# Acknowledgements

It was a pleasure to work with Michael Davern (undergraduate student at Wake Forest University, spring 2018) and with Peter Till (graduate student at Wake Forest University, fall 2017). Their class research project contributed to the research presented here in Chapter 3 and Chapter 4, respectively. They looked at a few hundred examples in authentic materials and textbooks to test the rules we had.

After three weeks in the semester, I knew that Michael had already accomplished the proficiency that most students should have at the end of the class. I proposed to him to work on a topic of his interest in lieu of the remaining regular assignments for the class. He chose *ser* and *estar*. As young folks say these days, he killed it. Of course, it took five times the time that I told him it would take us to write an article or chapter, but I have never heard a complaint from him. I am sure he will get the ambiguity in the last sentence. I remember that when we presented this work at a conference, he began by telling the audience that he would keep a leash on me during our presentation. He kept that promise. I have been putting up with that sense of humor since I met him.

A few other students (Will Biesel, Rebecca Buchanan, Landin Petersen) had looked at preterite and imperfect using Aktionsart classes to determine whether the choice of preterite/imperfect correlates with achievements, accomplishments, states, and activities, a distinction that will be explained in Chapter 4. Going through examples with Peter Till, I finally discovered that the same verb can express an accomplishment or an achievement, showing that Aktionsart is not really in the verb but in the sentence. Peter did the work that led me to abandon an Aktionsart explanation for preterite/ imperfect. I knew I had to look somewhere else. Working with Peter was as much fun as working with Michael. Bloody lovely!

My students Kyle Cattin, Audrey Dyer, and Savarni Sanka provided detailed comments for the whole manuscript. Sav asked me about the difference between restrictive and nonrestrictive adjectival clauses. I told her that I was going to try to explain the difference to someone without writing anything. I did it, and she understood. Several other students, colleagues, and friends have read at least one of these chapters and many of them have pointed out problems or suggested improvements. *¡Muchísimas gracias!*

My wife and my children have waited for me to get to things with great patience. Some of those things are still waiting. As I told Mary Friedman (my most loyal reader, not by her choosing), it takes me sometimes a couple of years to pay a promise, but I always try my best. My mother passed away in May 2020. I remember one day that there was a crisis at home and I told her that I would take care of it. She looked at me in the eyes as if asking me, "will you be able to deliver?" I told her, "I will not disappoint you, Mom". I did not disappoint her.

# Introduction

Examining four dichotomies in Spanish, this book shows how to reduce the six to ten rules common in textbooks for each contrast to a single binary distinction. That distinction is a form of totality vs. part, easier to see in some of the dichotomies, but present in all of them. A prenominal adjective, like a nonrestrictive adjectival clause, expresses totality; a postnominal adjective, like a restrictive adjectival clause, expresses part. The preterite expresses completeness, a form of totality; the imperfect expresses incompleteness; a form of part. *Ser/estar* express a similar total/part dichotomy.

An adjective preceding its noun in Spanish expresses a property shared by all of the referents of the noun (*los rápidos leones* 'the fast lions'; i.e. lions, which are fast). An adjective following its noun expresses a property shared only by some of the referents of the noun (*los animales carnívoros* 'animals that are carnivorous'). Likewise, a nonrestrictive adjectival clause expresses a property shared by all of the referents (often the only referent) of its <u>antecedent</u> (Gloria's <u>daughter</u>, who works in community outreach, is an urban planner). This sentence entails that Gloria has only one daughter. A restrictive adjectival clause expresses a property shared only by some of the referents of the <u>antecedent</u> (Gloria's <u>daughter</u>, the one who works in community outreach, is an urban planner). This sentence entails that Gloria has more than one daughter.

Why do native speakers use *estar* with sentences like the following: *el gato está afuera* 'the cat is outside'; *el gato está vacunado* 'the cat is vaccinated'; *el gato está jugando* 'the cat is playing'; *el gato está de buen humor* 'the cat is in a good mood'; *el gato está muerto* 'the cat is dead'? Why do they never say *\*el gato es afuera* 'the cat is outside'; *\*el gato es vacunado* 'the cat is vaccinated'; *\*el gato es jugando* 'the cat is playing'; *\*el gato es de buen humor* 'the cat is in a good mood'; *\*el gato es muerto* 'the cat is dead'? Why do they use *ser* but not *estar* in sentences like the following: *ese gato es nuestro* 'that cat is ours'; *ese gato es uno de los gaticos de Canela* 'that cat is one of Canela's kittens'; *ese gato es un* *gato doméstico* 'that cat is a domestic cat'; *ese es un gato angora* 'that is an Angora cat'; *ese gato es del vecino* 'that cat belongs to the neighbor'? Each of the sentences with *estar* expresses a change; none of those with *ser* does. Deep down, a state that does not change (or that rarely changes) is a totality; a state that changes is only a part.

The preterite and the imperfect are explained using the concept of interval in mathematics. A state or event expressed in the imperfect portrays a participant in the middle of an interval; the preterite signals that the participant entered or left the interval. This explanation is illustrated with the metaphor that the preterite is like entering or leaving a room (*empezó a llover* 'it began to rain'; *paró de llover* 'it stopped raining'); the imperfect is like staying in the room (*estábamos en casa* 'we were at home'; *llovía, pero no hacía frío* 'it was raining, but it was not cold'). This explanation shows what actions or states in progress, in the middle, ongoing, and repeated have in common: they all portray the participant at some point in the interval, without indicating when or whether the participant left it. This explanation also shows that the preterite is complete, signals a change, and is often punctual, all of them properties associated with the preterite. Deep down, the completeness of the preterite expresses totality; the incompleteness of the imperfect expresses part.

This book does not pretend to settle the discussion of the meaning of these four dichotomies. Its aim is to bring to the classroom scholars' current understanding of those dichotomies, and to do so in a way that students can understand and apply it in their learning of an L2. Each of these explanations has been tested in the teaching of Spanish as an L2 in college. Each explanation has also been presented at professional conferences during the last two decades.

Every chapter is example-driven; every assertion is drawn from or supported with examples. Many of the examples come from compositions written by college students, and readers have an opportunity to test out for themselves the explanation at work in the examples provided. Then, those examples are explained. In addition to examples from writing by students, there are examples from RAE (Real Academia Española y Asociación de Academias de la Lengua Española 'Royal Academy of the Spanish Language and Association of Academies of the Spanish Language'), from scholars, from writers, from Corpes XXI (RAE), from the Centro Virtual Cervantes, from the Internet, etc. Readers will see many of those examples presented as exercises, with answers provided. An additional brief explanation accompanies some of those answers, when appropriate.

Readers can see how the examples show the descriptive adequacy of each explanation, and how each explanation has predictive power. An explanation is descriptively adequate if it captures relevant generalizations in the data observed. An explanation has predictive power if it explains data not observed, not considered, or not available at the time it was formulated. The explanation in Bull (1965) that *estar* + a predicate adjective expresses change of state has predictive power because the same rule applies to three other rules for *estar*, and because it also explains putative idioms that turn out to express change of state. Something similar can be stated about each of the dichotomies studied in this book, since several rules are merged into a single distinction of totality/part.

A comparison of each of these explanations with those in textbooks shows that these explanations are simpler (Occam's razor), more predictive, and do not require ad hoc stipulations. These are three criteria discussed in Van Valin & LaPolla (1997: 5) to choose between competing analyses for a linguistic phenomenon. The same metrics apply to explanations in textbooks.

Although most of the teaching done now by this author is at the Intermediate and higher levels in the ACTFL scale (B1.1. and higher in the CEFR), an effort was made to give examples that could be understood by students at the elementary level.[1] In fact, the explanation on preterite/imperfect was applied to all of the examples given in an introductory textbook published in 2016 in the USA. Chapter 4 shows that the explanation proposed accounts for all of the examples given in the textbook's presentation of preterite/imperfect and in a short reading after that explanation (§4.5). That is evidence that the explanation proposed here can easily be incorporated into introductory textbooks. Examples taken from writing by students serve as a model for exercises beyond the elementary level; those taken from RAE and from Borges, for more advanced learners.

Not only are the six to ten rules for every dichotomy reduced to a more encompassing rule, but the main concept coded by each of these four dichotomies is the same: totality and part. Whole and part matters.

## Note

1 ACTFL is the American Council on the Teaching of Foreign Languages (www.actfl.org). CEFR is the Common European Frame of Reference for Languages (www.coe.int/en/web/common-european-framework-reference-languages).

# 1 Adjective position

## Why having a '*guapo novio*' does not raise any eyebrows, but having a '*novio guapo*' might

*Luis H. González*

## 1.1. Introduction

This chapter shows that adjective position in Spanish, a distinction that is difficult for native speakers and even for scholars, is a lot easier to understand with the distinction of nonrestrictive and restrictive adjectival clauses, a concept that is part of the grammar of English and many other languages. Section 2 explains that nonrestrictiveness expresses totality whereas restrictiveness expresses partitivity, and it explains this distinction with examples that show the concept in a way easily understood by college students. The examples come from scholars, from writers, from textbooks, from students, and from the Internet. Scholars have discussed similar – and sometimes identical examples. Many examples are presented as exercises throughout the chapter – and the book – with answers provided. Section 3 shows why an adjective modifying a noun with a single referent (a noun or a noun phrase that refers to a unique person, entity, or thing in the world) will precede that noun or noun phrase. That is the reason why speakers of Spanish should refer to their boyfriend as their *guapo novio* (their boyfriend, who is handsome) and not to their *novio guapo* (their boyfriend, the one who is handsome). Section 4 shows that scholars themselves have not understood well enough the concept of (non)restrictiveness and have resorted to word twisting, or have invoked subjectivity, value judgment attitude, affectedness, emphasis, etc., to try to explain some examples. Not only are all of those explanations unnecessary; they might be confusing. Sections 5 and 6 explain with plenty of examples the position of two adjectives modifying one noun. Examples from writing by the late J. L. Borges show that a reviewer or editor with the understanding of (non)restrictiveness proposed in this chapter might have asked J. L. Borges to consider the changes proposed in the answers to the exercises. Section 7 shows that the principle of linear modification in Bolinger (1952), which was meant as a theory of word order for language in general, helps in explaining (non)restrictiveness even better than scholars have thought until now. It also helps in understanding the position of two or more adjectives modifying a noun. Section 8 shows a prediction of this analysis that an undergraduate student discovered while in college. Section 9 shows that a better understanding of (non)restrictiveness makes it unnecessary to posit categories of adjectives that native speakers might not be aware of. Section 10 explains why many adjectives that are used clearly nonrestrictively and should precede the noun are used after the noun as a result of the omission of *que* + *ser* or *que* + *estar*. The adjective (or past participle) stays in situ when *que* + copular verb is omitted. Section 11 shows that a few adjectives in Spanish function as adverbs (*verdadero/a*) or might be a different word (i.e. a different part of speech) when used in one position or the other (*certain, simple, etc.*). Section 12 shows that totality vs. partitivity is a better explanation for some of the adjectives with a "difference in meaning" when used before or after the noun. In any case, the number of those pairs of *adjective* + *noun* or *noun* + *adjective* is lower than that in common lists. Section 13 briefly discusses some implications for teaching. Section 14 offers some conclusions.

Note: Specialized or key terms are capitalized when introduced or when they are very relevant for the point at hand. They are explained or exemplified as needed.

## 1.2. A <u>nonrestrictive</u> adjective expresses <u>totality</u>; a restrictive one expresses partitivity

Let us begin with one example that shows the difference between *guapo novio* 'a boyfriend, who is handsome', with the adjective preceding the noun and *novio **guapo*** 'a boyfriend that is handsome', with the adjective following it.[1]

(1)  a.  *el guapo novio de mi hermana*
         'my sister's boyfriend, who is a handsome person'
     b.  *el novio **guapo** de mi hermana*
         'my sister's boyfriend, the one who is handsome'

The difference is that in (1a), your sister has one boyfriend, and he is a handsome person. In (1b), your sister has at least two boyfriends, and only one of them is a handsome person. The phrase *guapo novio* in (1a) is nonrestrictive; the phrase *novio **guapo*** in (1b) is restrictive because it distinguishes from her boyfriends, the one who is handsome.

An adjective is <u>NONRESTRICTIVE</u> when the property that the adjective denotes (expresses) is a property of <u>ALL</u> of the nouns that the adjective *precedes*. An adjective is **RESTRICTIVE** when the property that the adjective denotes applies only to **PART** of the nouns that the adjective *follows*. Thus, a nonrestrictive adjective + noun (*guapo novio*) refers to the TOTALITY of the REFERENTS of the noun. A noun + **restrictive adjective** (*novio* **guapo**) refers to a **PART** of the referents of the noun. A witty definition of REFERENT in linguistics is that "a referent is what in the world a word refers to." The object that the reader has in their hands is the referent for the word *book*, if this is a physical book, not an ebook. Consider (2a–f):

(2) a. The actress Penélope Cruz, who is beautiful, is from Spain.
  b. #The actress Penélope Cruz that is beautiful is from Spain.[2]
  c. The beautiful Penélope Cruz (=2a)
  d. *The Penélope Cruz **beautiful** (=2b)[3]
  e. *La hermosa Penélope Cruz* (=2a)
  f. **La Penélope Cruz** ***hermosa*** (=2b)

The adjectival clause in (2a) – who is beautiful – is NONRESTRICTIVE. It tells the reader that Penélope Cruz has the property *beautiful* and, if omitted, the meaning of the sentence does not change. More importantly, having the property *beautiful* does not distinguish the Spanish actress Penélope Cruz from other Spanish actresses called Penélope Cruz. The adjectival clause in (2b) – that is beautiful – is RESTRICTIVE (if it were FELICITOUS). The information *that is beautiful* would in theory be needed to distinguish the actress Penélope Cruz that is beautiful from other Penélope Cruz-es that are actresses, and that are implied to be not beautiful. Let us define FELICITOUS:

> "In other words," says Mark Liberman, an instructor at the University of Pennsylvania, "a sentence must not only be grammatical to be correctly performed, it must also be felicitous," or well suited for the purpose.
>
> (Thought Company 2020)
> [Note: Mark Liberman is a famous professor and linguist.]

When a nonrestrictive adjective modifies a noun, it appears that Spanish looks like English. No speaker of English says *the Penélope Cruz beautiful* and no speaker of Spanish says *la Penélope Cruz hermosa*. Observe that (2a) is a sentence in English – and (2b) is not – because all of the Penélope Cruz-es that most people in the world know are beautiful. It is uncontroversial that most people in the world know only one Penélope Cruz, and most people will agree that she is a beautiful woman. Likewise, the string in (2e) is a string of words that speakers of Spanish produce and readily understand whereas (2f) is highly unlikely. A Google search in January 2018 for *la hermosa Penélope Cruz* and *la Penélope Cruz hermosa* returned 947 hits for the first string of words, and 0 for the second. English and Spanish align very well here. The problem is that Spanish requires many adjectives to go after the noun, and that is the reason for this chapter.

In short, the adjective *beautiful*, as applied to Penélope Cruz, the only Penélope Cruz that most people in the world know, is NONRESTRICTIVE. That means that for all purposes, all Penélope Cruz-es have the property beautiful, since there is only one. Most people in the world do not know any ugly Penélope Cruz.

To summarize, speakers of Spanish say *la hermosa Penélope Cruz* because *hermosa* is a property of the only Penélope Cruz that many people in the world know. That is, it applies to all of the possible referents for Penélope Cruz. Likewise, people should refer to their *guapo novio* and not to their *novio guapo* under the assumption that they have *only* one boyfriend.

A speaker of English (or a language in which the adjective precedes the noun) who is learning Spanish will be correct in assuming that the beautiful Penélope Cruz is *la hermosa Penélope Cruz*.[4] However, Spanish has many adjectives that can go after their noun when used restrictively and many others that must go after their noun because they are inherently restrictive.

Let us consider a case where the adjective must always go after the noun because it is necessarily RESTRICTIVE. The adjective *mexicano/a* 'Mexican' can be a property only of part of the nouns that it is a property of. This is true of any noun that can be modified by the adjective *mexicano/a*:

(3)  a.   the Mexican novelists
     b.   #the novelists Mexican
     c.   #*los mexicanos novelistas* (The "equivalent" in Spanish of 3b)
     d.   *los novelistas mexicanos* (The equivalent in Spanish of 3a)

*Mexican* was a property of over 128 million people in the world in February 2020. Furthermore, the number of novelists who have the property *Mexican* is a very small number of those 128 million.[5] Thus, the string *Mexican novelists* does not apply to all the novelists in the world; it does not even apply to all of the people in Mexico. It applies to a relatively small number of Mexicans. *Mexicano/a*, as applied to any noun in Spanish (and presumably in any language) is NECESSARILY RESTRICTIVE; that is, it means that for any noun at issue, the adjective *mexicano/a* refers to just a part of the referents of the noun. Therefore, the adjective *mexicanos/as* as applied to *novelistas*, selects from all the novelists in the world only those who are Mexican nationals. Due to the fact that *mexicanos/as* cannot be a property of all novelists, speakers of Spanish say *novelistas mexicanos/as* and they never say *\*mexicanos/as novelistas*. *Novelistas mexicanos/as* distinguishes novelists who are Mexican nationals from most novelists in the world, who are not Mexican novelists. The string of words *novelistas mexicanos/as* also DISTINGUISHES from the 128 million Mexican nationals the fraction of those Mexicans who are novelists. *Mexicano/a* is a RESTRICTIVE adjective because it restricts the meaning of *noun + mexicano/a* to only those nouns that also have the property *mexicano/a*.

We can now define a nonrestrictive and a restrictive adjective. Observe that if we use the word *precedes* and *follows* (instead of *modifies*), we are factoring in the rule of adjective position in Spanish without adding any words to the definition.

(4) Definition of nonrestrictive and restrictive adjectives:
   a. A <u>NONRESTRICTIVE</u> adjective expresses a property shared by *all* of the referents of the noun that the adjective *precedes*.[6]
   b. A **RESTRICTIVE** adjective expresses a property shared *only* by *some* of the referents of the noun that the adjective *follows*.

In other words, a RESTRICTIVE adjective expresses that the property *distinguishes* a sub-group of the referents of the noun from another group of the referents of the noun. In more specialized terms, a RESTRICTIVE adjective applies to a proper subset.[7] Nonrestrictiveness and restrictiveness also explain contrasts similar to the following one:

(5) a. *El hijo de Ana,* <u>el cual *estudió en New York University*</u>, *trabaja en Boston.*
      'Ana's son, *who* went to New York University, is working in Boston'.
   b. *El hijo de Ana,* **el que *estudió en New York University***, *trabaja en Boston.*
      'Ana's son, *the one who* went to New York University, is working in Boston'.

Since the series *el cual/la cual/las cuales/los cuales* is the nonrestrictive series in Spanish (Whitley & González 2016), (5a) refers to all of Ana's sons, who is her only son. Since the series *el que/la que/las que/los que* is the restrictive series, (5b) refers to part of Ana's sons. That is, (5b) entails that Ana has at least two sons. That is the difference in meaning between (5a) and (5b). The article in *el cual/el que* is not there to disambiguate between two possible "antecedents" with a different gender because the only antecedent is *hijo*. *De Ana* is a modifier, and the relative clause cannot refer to *de*

*Ana.* (The statement about "disambiguating" appears in eleven out of fifteen textbooks reviewed by Ozete 1981: 91).[8] Nor is *el cual* preferred due to a "motivo rítmico" (for rhythmic reasons) or because "pueden influir en ello preferencias individuales o regionales" (because there could be influences from individual or regional preferences), as Gili Gaya (1985[1961]: 307–308) proposed. There is a simpler and more encompassing explanation: it is just a matter of whole and part. Scholars (and interested readers) can verify that many (perhaps most) of the sentences with *el cual* are nonrestrictive, as Chapter 2 shows.

### 1.3. Why is *la hermosa Penélope Cruz* nonrestrictive and *los novelistas mexicanos* restrictive?

World knowledge matters (geography matters) and grammar matters. Singular and plural. A singular noun (the only referent) and a plural noun (two or more referents). Regarding nonrestrictiveness, there is a powerful prediction stemming from a noun with an ONLY REFERENT, as anticipated with *guapo novio*. If a noun refers to a single entity in the world (more precisely, in the universe of discourse), the adjective modifies all of the possible referents to which the noun refers. All of the possible referents is just one. Therefore, the adjective is necessarily nonrestrictive and it *precedes* the noun. On the other hand, plurality does not necessarily imply restrictiveness. Penélope Cruz's beautiful eyes are *los hermosos ojos de Penélope Cruz* and the captivating dances of the *Ballet Folklórico de México* are *las cautivadoras danzas del Ballet Folklórico de México*, under the assumption that all of their dances are captivating. An adjective that expresses a property that applies to all of the members of a set with two or more members will also be nonrestrictive. The following exercise will help in understanding nonrestrictiveness and restrictiveness.

**Exercise 1.** Determine which of the two strings of words makes sense and which one does not. If both make sense, explain the difference in meaning. Answers provided after the table.

Stop reading if you would like to think about the answers before reading about them.

*La amable Presidenta de ACTFL* means that there is only one ACTFL president at a time, and that she is a kind person. *La Presidenta amable de ACTFL* would mean that there are at least two presidents of ACTFL, and that only one of them is a kind person. The first sentence is more likely than the second one. *Los ojos hermosos de Sara* 'Sara's eyes, the ones that are beautiful' would mean that she has some eyes that are beautiful and other eyes that are not. The correct answer is *los hermosos ojos de Sara. Las*

*Table 1.1* Exercise 1

| | |
|---|---|
| La amable Presidenta de ACTFL | La Presidenta amable de ACTFL |
| Los hermosos ojos de Sara | Los ojos hermosos de Sara |
| Las impresionantes Cataratas de Iguazú | Las Cataratas de Iguazú impresionantes |
| El ardiente calor de julio en Miami | El calor ardiente de julio en Miami |
| Las frías noches de enero en Canadá | Las noches frías de febrero en Georgia, EE.UU. |
| Los blancos cabellos del abuelo | Los cabellos blancos del abuelo |
| La nocturna vida de Nueva York | La vida nocturna de Nueva York |
| La interesante vida nocturna de Nueva York | La vida nocturna interesante de Nueva York |

*cataratas impresionantes de Iguazú* 'the Iguazú falls that are impressive' implies that there are several *cataratas de Iguazú* and only some of them are impressive. The answer is *las impresionantes cataratas de Iguazú*. Thus, the first three examples are nonrestrictive because the adjective refers to all of the referents of ACTFL's current President, Sara's eyes, and the Iguazú falls. *El ardiente sol de julio en Miami* 'July's burning sun in Miami' means that most, if not all days in July are very hot in Miami. If we agree that all nights in January in Canada will be cold, then it is *las frías noches de enero en Canadá* 'the cold nights in January in Canada' (the nights in January in Canada, which are all cold). However, if we move south to the state of Georgia in the USA a month later, then it is possible that some nights in February will be cold and some will not be cold; hence, *las noches **frías** de febrero* is probably correct for most Februaries in Georgia, USA. *Los blancos cabellos del abuelo* means that all of grandpa's hair is white. *Los cabellos **blancos** del abuelo* means that he has some white hair and some hair that is not white. *La vida **nocturna** de NYC* contrasts with the day life in NYC. *Nocturna* is necessarily restrictive as applied to life in Spanish –it contrasts at least with day life. No speaker of Spanish will say *la nocturna vida de NYC*.[9] Many people agree that night life in NYC. is interesting; therefore, *la interesante vida **nocturna** de NYC*.

## 1.4. With nonrestrictiveness and restrictiveness, there is no need for word twisting, for explanations that do not make sense (6 below), or for invoking emphasis, subjectivity, affectedness, value judgments

Now that readers have a good grasp of nonrestrictiveness and restrictiveness, they can evaluate the following phrases and the explanation for each in Dozier & Iguina (2017: 39). These are four out of their seven examples.

(6) a.  el *extravagante* Dalí
        'the extravagant Salvador Dalí' (Salvador Dalí was extravagant by
        nature)
    b.  la *conocida* profesora Sainz
        'the well-known professor Sainz' (her fame precedes her)
    c.  tu *pequeño* ombligo
        'your small navel' (smallness is an inherent property of your navel)
    d.  mi *hermosa* madre
        'my beautiful mother' (my mother is innately beautiful)

There are four different explanations for the same pattern. Each of those nouns is singular; therefore, the adjective should be nonrestrictive and prenominal. The explanation for each of the phrases in (6a–d) should be the same, and it is. There is only one Salvador Dalí that most people in the world will uniquely identify, he was an extravagant man, and he is without a doubt the Salvador Dalí intended in the example. There is no other Dalí known by many people in the world who is not extravagant (cf. #*el Salvador Dalí extravagante* '#Salvador Dalí, the one who was extravagant'). We can be sure that the authors were thinking of the only professor Sainz at their university (where they work now, or the university that they attended and where they were acquainted with the well-known professor Sainz that they have in mind and are honoring with this example). Dozier & Iguina are not referring to any other professors Sainz who are not well-known. Every person has just one navel, and, apparently, the listener's navel in their example is small. If one were to say that *su sucio ombligo contribuyó a la infección* 'her/his dirty navel contributed to the infection', *dirty* cannot be an inherent *property* of the navel. However, if that navel was dirty, speakers of Spanish should say *sucio ombligo* and not *ombligo **sucio***, because if they were to say *el ombligo **sucio** contribuyó a la infección*, they would be implying that the person has a dirty navel and at least another one that is not dirty. *Extravagante, conocida, pequeño*, and *hermosa* precede their corresponding noun because they denote a property shared by all of the referents (a singular referent in each case) that the noun denotes. That is the same explanation not only for (6a–d), but also for an infinite number of nouns with just one referent.

An adjective that precedes its noun does so more because it is nonrestrictive than because it is inherent. An inherent property is nonrestrictive, but a nonrestrictive property is not necessarily inherent. The property *dirty* as applied to your only navel is not inherent, but it is nonrestrictive.

Readers can also determine whether the following explanations make much sense. Are the explanations for (7b,d,f) really relevant and useful? This author is a native speaker, and believes that (7b,d,f) are uninterpretable, to put it mildly.

(7)  a.  *una respuesta **falsa**: no ajustada a la verdad* (RAE 2010: 257)
      'an answer that is false: not adjusted to the truth'
   b.  *una <u>falsa</u> respuesta: que lo es falsamente* (RAE 2010: 257)
      'a false answer: that it is so, falsely'
   c.  *un negocio **simple**: no complejo* (RAE 2010: 257)
      'a business/issue that is simple: not complex'
   d.  *un <u>simple</u> negocio: que no es otra cosa, que lo es simplemente* (RAE 2010: 257)
      'a simple business/issue: that it is not another thing; that it is so, simply'
   e.  *un testimonio **verdadero**: veraz, cierto* (=True). (RAE 2010: 257)
      'a testimony that is true: veracious, true'
   f.  *un <u>verdadero</u> testimonio: que lo es verdaderamente* (RAE 2010: 257)
      'a true testimony: that it truly is'

The examples and glosses in (7) show that RAE, which adopts the non-restrictiveness and restrictiveness distinction (RAE 2010: 238), is not applying it consistently; and, like Bello, fails to see the predictions of the explanation that they are using. The reader will understand better the problems in the preceding examples with the help of the following one:

(8)  a.  *una verdadera noticia* (0.0000013457%, Ngram Viewer, August 2019)
   b.  *una noticia verdadera* (0.0000007895%, Ngram Viewer, August 2019)

The frequency for *noticia verdadera* is 58.49% of that for *verdadera noticia*, according to the Ngram Viewer (2020). A *noticia verdadera* 'true news' would be 'a piece of news that is true'. That does not make much sense because if a piece of news is not true, it is not news, it is a lie. Thus, *noticia verdadera* should not be a string of words in Spanish (nor should be *falsa respuesta* in 7b above). On the other hand, *verdadera noticia* is a case of a false cognate. A *verdadera noticia* is an *important* piece of news, a piece of news worth of full attention. *Verdadera noticia* is similar to the collocation *cantar lindo*[adjective] instead of *cantar lindamente*[adverb] 'sing beautifully'. *Verdadera noticia* is similar to the string *crazy rich* in English, in which *crazy* is not an adjective but an adverb. A book by Kevin Kwan (2013) titled *Crazy Rich Asians* was translated into Spanish as *Locos, ricos y asiáticos* (2018). *Asiáticos absurdamente ricos* (i.e. *locamente ricos*) would have been a better translation. Those who have read the book (or at least seen the movie) would agree that this title reflects better the spirit of the book than *Locos, ricos y asiáticos*, a good translation for crazy, rich, and Asians, but not the title of the book. Punctuation matters. Part of speech matters. The position of the adjective matters because it is meaningful.

Readers will also be able to determine whether both of the following phrases make sense or only one of them does:

(9)  a.  *Este es un <u>verdadero</u> problema.*
         'This is a serious (not trivial) problem'.
     b.  *Este es un problema verdadero.*
         '#This is a problem that is true'.

Only one of them makes sense: the one that means that this is a serious problem. Not the one that would mean that this problem is true, not false. The answer to a problem (a math problem) is true or not true, but that is another problem. If some readers are not yet convinced, the following examples should help. The sentences are from best to worst:

(10) a.  *Austin es una ciudad verdaderamente internacional.*
         'Austin is a truly international city'.
     b.  *Austin es una ciudad internacional de verdad.*[10]
         %'Austin is a true international city'.
     c.  #Austin es una ciudad internacional verdadera.
         '#Austin is an international true city'.

Returning to the sentences in (7) above, one reads in RAE (1973: 410):

> El adjetivo que se anticipa denota, pues, actitud valorativa y afectiva; por esto es muy frecuente en oraciones exclamativas, o en las que están más o menos teñidas de estimaciones y sentimientos: *¡Bonita casa!, ¡El cochino dinero tiene la culpa de todo!, Magnífica ocasión para hablarle, Vivía torturado por la insufrible espera de noticias.*
>
> 'The adjective that precedes denotes, then, a valorative, an affective attitude; because of this it is very frequent in exclamations, or in those sentences that are more or less tainted with affections and feelings: *Beautiful house!; Money, which is dirty, is to blame for everything!; Magnificent occasion to talk to her/him; He lived tortured by the unbearable wait for news'.*
>
> (Translation by the author)

A similar statement is found in RAE (2009: 997). Nonrestrictiveness predicts that this is exactly how speakers should express the adjectives. Furthermore, there is no need to invoke subjectivity or any expression of affection (or any relevant affectedness) when a guest is invited to a house that the guest finds gorgeous, and proceeds to offer a compliment to the host by stating how beautiful it is. The use of *cochino* 'dirty' as a property of money is a well-established property in the sense that too much of it often corrupts. Nonrestrictiveness clearly explains the sarcastic reading for *magnificent occasion to talk to her/him*(!), the most likely interpretation for this sentence. With the notion of nonrestrictiveness, there is no need for any of these explanations. Each of those nouns has a single referent. Nonrestrictiveness predicts that the adjective should precede. Furthermore, an adjective that follows the noun will result in a distortion of the meaning. In the sense intended, there is no other house; therefore, it cannot be not beautiful; there is no clean money (when there is too much of it); there is no other wait; therefore, it cannot be bearable; etc.

This section has shown that with a better understanding of (non)restrictiveness, there is no need to propose different explanations for the same pattern. If we agree that *noticia verdadera* does not make sense, but that a <u>*verdadera*</u> *noticia* is a 'truly important piece of news', RAE (2010: 257) is on the right track when it states that the adjective *verdadero* is functioning like an adverb. The fact that an adjective can function as an adverb is attested both in Spanish and in English. A dictionary of English need not be crazy good to have an entry for *crazy* as an adverb.

## 1.5. Two adjectives modifying a noun

If many adjectives can be either nonrestrictive or restrictive, then with two adjectives, the possibilities are that both are nonrestrictive, one of them is nonrestrictive and the other is restrictive, or both of them are restrictive. All of those possibilities are attested. A further question arises. If both adjectives precede or follow, do they go in any order? Sections 5 to 8 answer all of these questions.

The translator into Spanish of one of Carl Sagan's books (*The demon-haunted world: Science as a candle in the dark*, 1995. Penguin Random House, LLC) incorrectly translated a noun with two adjectives. The following phrases show the possible combinations. With the understanding of (non)restrictiveness that readers have gained, they will be able to determine which of the following phrases is the only one that is correct. (Non)restrictiveness predicts it. It is also possible to predict what Sagan wrote, if he wrote what he most probably meant. It must have been *chaotic cosmic violence*, as will be clearer after §1.7.

(11) a. *la caótica cósmica violencia*
    b. *la cósmica caótica violencia*
    c. *la violencia cósmica caótica*
    d. *la violencia caótica cósmica*
    e. *la caótica violencia cósmica*
    f. *la cósmica violencia caótica*

The translator must have translated the sentence as (11c) or (11d). Both are incorrect. There are several types of violence: animal, criminal, domestic, state, street, etc. *Cósmica* is one type of violence. Therefore, *cósmica*, as applied to violence is restrictive. It can only be *violencia cósmica*. Readers should have not read or heard *la cósmica violencia*. The next question is, is *caótica*, referring to *violencia cósmica*, nonrestrictive or restrictive? All cosmic violence is chaotic. Therefore, it must be *la caótica violencia cósmica*, as (non)restrictiveness predicts for two, three, four, or more adjectives. And without invoking the notion of "more important adjective" or "the one that carries more information", notions that are difficult, if not impossible to define. If "more information" is measurable, it will be somewhat difficult to do so because it will be on a continuum. On the other hand, (non)restrictiveness is a lot easier to measure because it is a matter of *yes* or *no*. Indeed, with (non)restrictiveness, there is no need to invoke these notions (an adjective that is more important or the one that carries more information), as the rest of this chapter will show. To summarize, a good understanding of restrictiveness allows speakers of Spanish to predict exactly what the translator should have written. Likewise, speakers of English will be able to predict exactly what Sagan wrote.

The notion of epithets, particularly short ones, has led to some misconceptions that go back to Bello (1941[1847]: 12):

> Lo más común en castellano es anteponer al sustantivo los epítetos cortos y posponerle los adjetivos especificantes, como se ve en *mansas ovejas* y *animales mansos*, pero este orden se invierte a menudo, principalmente en verso.
>
> The most common practice in Castillian is to place before the noun short epithets and place after the noun specifying adjectives, as can be seen in *tame sheep* and *tame animals*, but this order is often reversed, mainly in verse.
>
> (Translation by the author)

Observe that Bello got lost in his own example (he did not use a short adjective before the noun and a longer one after). It is true that *mansos* must follow *animals* because all animals are not tame. We can also concede to him that sheep are tame, in general.

The observation that epithets commonly precede their noun when they are short has been repeated for over 150 years. The following underlined text looks like an epithet, although it should not precede the noun on the account of not being short: *Apareció en el tejado el <u>delirante pero incomparablemente paranoico-ingenioso</u> pintor don Salvador Dalí* 'There appeared on the roof the delirant but uncomparably paranoic-ingenious painter Mr. Salvador Dalí'. Both the quote and its translation are from Thompson (2020), who goes on to explain that, "a ridiculously long adjectival phrase is forced between *el* and *pintor*, but this is obviously for extravagant stylistic effect". It is not extravagant stylistic effect. These descriptive adjectives are all nonrestrictive when applied to Dalí. This is not extravagant writing. Whoever wrote that sentence about Dalí is a writer with a good intuition of the language.

There is a statement in pedagogical materials for Spanish that if two adjectives modify a noun, the shortest or less important one precedes the noun (Rule 1). Or both adjectives can go together with the conjunction *y* 'and' in Spanish, as when speakers of the language will refer to 'a tall, beautiful girl' as *una chica alta y hermosa* (Rule 2).

Thus, if we wanted to put together the words *alta, esposa de George Clooney, hermosa* (in alphabetical order), 'tall, George Clooney's wife, beautiful' in a phrase, and we followed the two rules in the preceding paragraph, these are the possibilities:

(12) a.  *la <u>alta</u> esposa **hermosa** de George Clooney* (By Rule 1, shorter adjective preceding)
  b.  *la <u>hermosa</u> esposa **alta** de George Clooney*
     (By Rule 1, assuming that *hermosa* is less important than *alta*)
  c.  *la esposa **alta** y **hermosa** de George Clooney* (By Rule 2)

*all wrong*

None of these sentences are correct, they all imply that George Clooney has more than one wife, and they fail to communicate that George Clooney's only wife is *la <u>alta</u> y <u>hermosa</u> Amal Clooney* 'the tall, beautiful Amal Clooney'. Incidentally, could she be *la <u>hermosa</u> y <u>alta</u> Amal*? Yes, because (prenominal) *nonrestrictive* descriptive adjectives are UNORDERED in Spanish and in English – except if they are determiners and quantifiers. (See Pérez-Leroux et al. 2020, for a discussion of ordering that factors in determiners and quantifiers).[11] Crucially, prenominal nonrestrictive adjectives require the conjunction *and* and commas, if more than two, in both languages. The reader should observe that *prenominal* is not needed in the phrase *nonrestrictive descriptive adjectives* with the understanding of (non) restrictiveness advanced in this chapter.

Consider the following statements about the Clooneys' daughters, who are twin girls. The author hopes the Clooneys will excuse this intrusion into their lives. We use these examples simply because they help learners of Spanish (not only as an L2 but also as an L1) understand a point poorly understood until now. At the time of the writing of this chapter, the Clooneys had two twin girls.

(13) a.   las <u>hermosas</u> gemelas de Amal y George
       'Amal and George's beatutiful twins'
   b.   las gemelas **hermosas** de Amal y George
   c.   la gemela **hermosa** de Amal y George
   d.   la <u>hermosa</u> gemela de Amal y George

If we know that the Clooneys have just one set of twin daughters, which sentence correctly expresses that state of affairs, (13a) or (13b)? (13a). What would (13b–d) mean if they were true? The reader will find the answers after the next paragraph.

Is this the <u>emocionante</u> capítulo **interesante** *sobre la posición del adjetivo*? ('the exciting and interesting chapter about adjective position'). Or is it the <u>interesante</u> capítulo **emocionante**? Wait! Both adjectives are equally long. Or is one of the adjectives more important than the other? That decision will not be free from controversy, though. That is also a dead end. Then, can we go with the *capítulo* **interesante** *y* **emocionante**? No author would go for that order because it would imply that there is another chapter on adjective position that is boring and not exciting. Why write a boring and unexciting chapter if you have already written one that is interesting and exciting? Is there any way to put together these two adjectives with the noun *capítulo*? There sure is. If there is only one chapter on adjective position, and if *interesting* and *exciting* are properties that apply to it, then this must be the <u>emocionante</u> e <u>interesante</u> *capítulo sobre la posición del adjetivo*. It is exactly that. Nothing more, nothing less. As predicted by nonrestrictiveness, and the fact that there is only one chapter on adjective position in this book. Actually, nonrestrictiveness predicts that if *emocionante* and *interesante* are properties of all of the referents of *este capítulo*, then this chapter can also be called the *interesante y emocionante capítulo sobre la posición del adjetivo*. We will briefly make a further connection with this example at the end of §1.8.

Here are the answers to the questions about the sentences referring to the Clooney twins. *Las gemelas **hermosas** de Amal y George* (13b) would mean that the Clooneys have at least two sets of twins, and at least one of the twins is not beautiful. *La gemela **hermosa** de Amal y George* (13c) would mean that only one of the two twins is beautiful. *La <u>hermosa</u> gemela* *de Amal y George* (13d) would mean that there is only one twin left. This author wishes the best to the Clooneys, and hopes the twins grow up to read these examples as a sign of admiration for the Clooneys, who are truly intelligent, compassionate, generous, and handsome people with a good sense of humor (*gente verdaderamente inteligente, compasiva, generosa, guapa y con un buen sentido del humor*).

**Exercise 2.** The following phrases or sentences come from the late J. L. Borges, an Argentinian writer. Would the reader suggest any changes after the explanation so far? As Borges himself would have probably written, it would not be unreasonable to conjecture that Borges was not aware – explicitly – of nonrestrictiveness and restrictiveness. There is a brief explanation after the exercise. The number in parentheses is the page number in Borges (1974).

1. […] *los negros y dorados LOMOS de la Anglo-American Cyclopaedia* (433)
2. *leí estas curiosas PALABRAS* (434)
3. *reconstruir los muchos y macizos TOMOS que faltan* (434)
4. *una irresponsable LICENCIA de la imaginación* (435)
5. *ese arriesgado CÓMPUTO nos retrae al* […] (434)
6. *hay poemas famosos compuestos de una sola enorme PALABRA* (436)
7. *dos términos, uno de* […] *otro auditivo:* […] *y el remoto GRITO de un pájaro* (435)
8. *la paradójica verdad es que existen, en casi innumerable NÚMERO* (436)
9. […] *o sea el caso hipotético de nueve hombres que en nueve sucesivas NOCHES padecen un vivo DOLOR* (438)
10. *denunciaron la pérfida CIRCUNSTANCIA algo herrumbradas por la lluvia del miércoles,* […] (438)

All of the adjectives (in Spanish) in the previous phrases or sentences are nonrestrictive and they are correctly used prenominally. The property denoted by the adjective applies to all of the referents that the noun denotes. Or it applies to the only referent, when there is only one referent, which happens eight times out of 12. But nothing should be read from that frequency. Readers will have noticed, however, that two sentences had two prenominal adjectives modifying a noun. Both of those adjectives are nonrestrictive and they are conjoined with *y* 'and'. They are on the other side of the example of the *chica alta y bonita*. If this author is a woman, then her husband will be *su alto y guapo esposo* and not *su esposo alto y guapo*. Unless the author has more than one spouse. That is not the case.

**Exercise 3.** This set of phrases or sentences is also from J. L. Borges. This time, some changes are called for. Some of the adjectives are nonrestrictive and they should precede their noun. Interestingly, native speakers often use nonrestrictive adjectives after its noun. However, it is extremely rare to find a restrictive adjective preceding a noun. §1.10 explains why many nonrestrictive adjectives are used after their noun.

Let us turn our attention back to the exercise. Answers will be provided right after the exercise. Remember that the number in parentheses is the page number in Borges (1974).

1. *desde el FONDO **remoto** del corredor* [...] (431)
2. *el EXAMEN **estéril** de uno de los atlas de Justus Perthes* [...] (431)
3. *[...] entre las <u>efusivas</u> MADRESELVAS y el FONDO **ilusorio** de los espejos* [...] (433)
4. *algún RECUERDO **limitado y menguante** de Herbert Ashe, ingeniero de los ferrocarriles* [...] (433)
5. *[...] mirando a veces los COLORES **irrecuperables** del cielo* [...] (433)
6. *me puse a hojearlo y sentí un VÉRTIGO **asombrado y ligero** que no describiré* [...] (434)
7. *básteme recordar que las CONTRADICCIONES **aparentes** del onceno tomo* [...] (435)
8. *[...] yo pienso que sus TIGRES **transparentes** y sus torres de sangre no merecen* [...] (435)
9. *el mundo para ellos no es un concurso de objetos en el espacio; es una SERIE **heterogénea** de actos independientes.* (435)

Answers: All of the 11 adjective(s) in bold should precede their noun, as *efusivas* does.

1. El <u>remoto</u> fondo del corredor. There is only one "far end of a hallway", as it is also clear in the translation into English: "The mirror troubled *the far end* of a hallway in a large country house" (Borges 1998: 68). And that end is *remoto* 'far'. (The reader will remember 'el <u>remoto</u> grito de un pájaro' in example 7 above, from Borges himself).
2. There was one exam of the atlas, and it was sterile.
3. Entre las efusivas madreselvas y el fondo ilusorio de los espejos. *Efusivas madreselvas* is correct. But it should be the <u>*ilusorio* fondo</u> *de los espejos*. Mirrors have only one *fondo*, and it is illusory.[12] Regardless of whether one goes with the Spanish *ilusorio fondo de los espejos* (as I conjecture an editor with a good understanding of (non)restrictiveness would have suggested) or the English *illusory depths of the mirrors* from the translation into English, the adjective

should precede. Notice that the translator also made plural the noun *fondo* 'depths'.

4. It should be "Algún limitado y menguante recuerdo de Herbert Ashe [...]" There was only one memory; therefore the adjectives should precede.
5. Mirando a veces los irrecuperables colores del cielo [...]. All of the colors of a beautiful sunset, the interpretation intended, are irrecoverable. ("[...] holding a book of mathematics, looking up sometimes at the irrecoverable colors of the sky" (Borges 1998: 71)).
6. It should be "Sentí un asombrado y ligero vértigo que no describiré".
7. It should be "Básteme recordar las aparentes contradicciones del onceno tomo [...]"
8. It should be "[...] yo pienso que sus transparentes tigres y sus torres de sangre [...]", under the assumption that all of the tigers are transparent, which appears to be the intended reading.
9. It should be "En una heterogénea serie de actos [...]" There is just one series of acts, and it is heterogeneous.

This author presented this explanation at an informal college gathering of colleagues in linguistics and literature from several language departments circa 2008 (The Linguistics Circle, Wake Forest University). When the second set of Borges examples were discussed, an attendee asked, "are you telling us that native speakers make mistakes, let alone a writer like J. L. Borges?" The answer from this author was that if he/she had been Borges' editor, he/she would have suggested the corrections discussed above. As Borges himself would have written, the conjecture that Borges would have accepted those suggestions would not be unreasonable. Indeed, there is evidence from his own writing that he would have written the sentences in exercise 3 as suggested in the answers provided. That evidence is all of the sentences in exercise 2.

## 1.6. Is Italian red wine different from red Italian wine?

Yes, if we are in front of at least two different wines.[13] Bolinger (1954: 52) explained the difference as follows:

> Furthermore, when there are no parentheses a series will give step-by-step narrowings: vino rojo italiano is primarily about "vino rojo" which happens to be "italiano"; while vino italiano rojo is primarily "vino italiano" narrowed, for this particular occasion to "rojo."

With a better understanding of restrictiveness, we can explain it as follows. *Vino rojo italiano* 'Italian red wine' means that we have *red wines* from different countries, and this one is from Italy. *Vino italiano rojo* 'red Italian wine' means that we have different types of *Italian wines*, and this one is red; not white, burgundy, gray, orange, rosé, sangria, tawny, verde, yellow, etc.

(14) a.   Italian[2] red[1] wine = *vino rojo*[1] *italiano*[2]
     b.   Red[2] Italian[1] wine = *vino italiano*[1] *rojo*[2]

## 1.7. Bolinger (1952: 1118) principle of linear modification … modified

Let us start with an exercise in English, and its translation into Spanish.

**Exercise 4.** The following words are in alphabetical order. In the correct order, they form a determiner phrase (= a noun phrase). A determiner phrase is a noun and its prenominal modifiers (articles, demonstrative adjectives, possessive adjectives, quantifiers, adjectives, etc.) and its postnominal modifiers (adjectives, prepositional phrases, adjectival clauses, etc.). Most of the words in the following exercise are nouns. In each phrase, only one of them is functioning as a noun. The rest of those nouns are functioning as adjectives. Observe the two examples before you do the exercise.

Example 1. #Earrings, golden. Ordered as a real-world phrase: golden earrings 'aretes de oro'.
Example 2: #Chicago, Concert, Orchestra, Symphony: Chicago Symphony Orchestra Concert 'Concierto de la Orquesta Sinfónica de Chicago'.

Here is the exercise. Grab a piece of paper and try to write a string of words that makes sense by putting together the following words in a correct order. Do not read below the quote by Bolinger if you would like to do the exercise before looking at the answer. You can, however, read up to the quote for some help.

(15) airbag, campaign, Corolla, indicator, malfunction, lamp, service, special

---

If you know some Spanish, try to translate it. In Spanish, you will need to add five prepositions (the same preposition five times). You will also need to use a definite article (the equivalent in Spanish of *the*) three times.

---

If you feel a little lost, observe the translation into Spanish of *Chicago Symphony Orchestra Concert* below. Hint: look at the word order. Readers will see the answer after this quote from Bolinger (1952: 1118), where he states his principle of linear modification:

> Let us consider what happens when elements – call them words, for convenience – are laid end-to-end to form a phrase. Before the speaker begins, the possibilities of what he will communicate are practically infinite, or, if his utterance is bound within a discourse, they are at least enormously large. When the first word appears, the possibilities are vastly reduced, but that first word has, in communicative value for the hearer, its fullest possible semantic range. The second word follows, narrowing the range, the third comes to narrow it still further, and finally the end is reached at which point the sentence presumably focuses on an event usually aided by a gesture, a physical context in which only one of several possibilities can be elected, or what-not.

Here is the answer to the exercise and its translation into Spanish:

(16) Corolla airbag malfunction indicator light special service campaign.
(17) Campaña de servicio especial de la luz indicadora de desperfecto de la bolsa de aire del Corolla.

Which is the noun functioning like a noun? *Campaign*. The other nouns are functioning like an adjective of the nouns with which they are associated.

It is also interesting that the first word in English is the last one in Spanish and vice versa. In fact, the whole phrase in Spanish is a mirror image of the one in English, except for the prepositions and articles needed in Spanish.[14]

Bolinger's principle of linear modification was meant as a principle of word order for any language. He was a scholar who pursued the big picture. It is true that the first word in an utterance begins to restrict the meaning of the sentence (or phrase) that is coming, and as words are added to that utterance, the more restrictive each word is, and the more narrowed down the possible meaning becomes until an event is focused on. It is clear that Bolinger's principle helped other scholars (Bolinger 1952, 1954; Cressey 1969; RAE 2010; Solé & Solé 1977; Stockwell et al. 1965; Whitley 2002; among others) grasp the intuition of restrictiveness to the right, as Terker (1985: 505) noted. We must re-think linear modification in order to accommodate restrictiveness to the left in English. However, restrictiveness can explain it. We simply have to factor in polarity (right to left instead of left to right). All languages have polarity in several dimensions. Thus, we will have to modify Bolinger's principle of linear modification, but restrictiveness does not have to. This suggests that restrictiveness is sufficient, and linear modification is, therefore, not necessary. Granted, restrictive and nonrestrictive adjectival clauses would have led scholars to figure out restrictiveness, but it is undeniable that Bolinger's insight sped up that understanding. An exploration of the understanding of (non)restrictiveness before Bolinger and after him might shed light on this issue.

Solé & Solé (1977) observed that the rightmost adjective is the most restrictive in Spanish, an observation that was most probably inspired by Bolinger's principle. That explanation solves several problems observed by several scholars (Fábregas 2017; Marín 2016; RAE 2010; Terker 1985; Whitley 2002; among many others). By looking at the Corolla airbag example in English and its equivalent in Spanish, we can put together Solé & Solé's observation with polarity (left to right ever increasing restrictiveness) in order to get a highly predictive explanation for adjective position in Spanish. And in *English*.

(18) In Spanish, the more to the right of its noun an adjective is, the more restrictive it is.

It turns out that a similar principle is at work in English, but to the left of the noun:

(19) In English, the more to the left of its noun an adjective is, the more restrictive it is.[15]

Two important observations follow from the *Corolla airbag* phrase. First, restrictiveness is not necessarily more information, as Stockwell et al. (1965: 89) suggest when they state that, "the item in final position carries more information". Determining with enough precision what "more information" is might be a challenge. In Spanish, an adjective to the right of another narrows a step further the referents of the noun + adjective(s) preceding it. In fact, the rightmost adjective selects a subset (a part) of the referents expressed by the noun + adjective(s) to its left. Furthermore, the notion of "more information" is difficult, if not impossible to quantify. If "more information" is measurable, it will be so on a continuum. On the other hand, (non)restrictiveness is not only discrete (counted in integers); it is *binary*, as the examples discussed so far have shown. Second, prenominal position is neither more emphatic nor is it more "subjective" or "affected-like". It is simply nonrestrictiveness (i.e. totality). Those perceptions of emphasis, subjectivity, affectedness come from several factors. First, nonrestrictiveness might be the marked option for many adjectives.[16] Second, it has a flair of literariness to it. Prenominal adjectives seem hyperbaton-like. The literariness of a marked (atypical) chain of words is a provocative issue for further research. Luis de Góngora and J. L. Borges come to mind as writers with whom to start.

If a restrictive adjective follows the noun, and the more to the right an adjective is, the more restrictive it is, the order of each adjective codes a difference in meaning, as the example about *Italian red wine* or *red Italian wine* shows, even in English – but to the left of the noun, of course. On the other hand, adjectives that precede the noun are nonrestrictive. Crucially, a more restrictive adjective cannot be conjoined with a conjunction to the following adjective. However, we saw that the *alta y hermosa Amal Clooney* requires the conjunction *y*. We also know that both properties apply to all of the Amal Clooneys that many people in the world know. In fact, if we wanted to add a further property to Amal Clooney, we could say, for example:

(20) *la alta, hermosa e inteligente Amal Clooney*
'the tall, beautiful, and intelligent Amal Clooney'

By the way, this example is similar to one from Terker (1985: 505):

(21) *Quiero ante todo agradecer muy sinceramente las ELOGIOSAS, AMABLES, y TAN CARIÑOSAS palabras que me han dedicado.*
'Before anything, I want to give sincere thanks for the laudable, kind, and so affectionate words that have been dedicated to me'.

As Terker himself observes, these three adjectives can go in any order. That is exactly as nonrestrictiveness predicts by virtue of the fact that those adjectives are properties of all of the referents of the noun that they precede. Crucially, two prenominal adjectives in Spanish require a conjunction; three or more require comma(s) and a conjunction. Interestingly, English also requires comma(s) and a conjunction when two or more adjectives are nonrestrictive. Punctuation matters.

## 1.8. Allie Neal's prediction regarding determiners and quantifiers before a noun

As an undergraduate student, Allie Neal explored adjective position in Spanish, and how it should find its way into L2 textbooks. She discovered a prediction of this analysis that had not occurred to this author. She realized that DETERMINERS (articles, demonstrative adjectives, possessive adjectives) and QUANTIFIERS (expressions of quantity before a noun) are nonrestrictive because they refer to all of the referents to which the determiner or quantifier and the noun refer. Notice that the examples are in English. Of course, these determiner phrases (noun phrases) are nonrestrictive in Spanish as well.

(22) a.  <u>_These_</u> examples will help students a lot.
  b.  <u>_Fifty_</u> pages explain <u>_a_</u> dichotomy in some detail.
  c.  <u>_My_</u> brothers and sisters live in <u>_two_</u> different cities.
  d.  <u>_My eight_</u> brothers and sisters live in <u>_two_</u> different cities.
  e.  <u>_Some_</u> students were wearing <u>_their_</u> college's t-shirts.
  f.  <u>_The first three exciting and interesting Spanish grammar_</u> chapters.
      '<u>Los tres primeros emocionantes e interesantes</u> capítulos de la gramática del español'.

The preceding explanation by Allie Neal helps in understanding why the last three of the five classes of adjectives in Demonte (1999) to be discussed at the end of the following section are nonrestrictive (circumstancials [temporal, locative, manner], aspectual, and intensional). It is also clear why descriptive (_cielo **azul**_ 'blue sky') and relational adjectives (_puerto **marítimo**_ 'sea port', _vaca **lechera**_ 'milking cow') are restrictive. The latter are simply "type of noun". Hence, they are restrictive, and therefore postnominal. Allie Neal's prediction also explains several of the adjectives with "a different meaning" discussed in §1.12. Several of those adjectives are quantifiers or determiners. They denote a totality when prenominal: _<u>cierto</u> hombre tocó la puerta_ 'certain man knocked on the door'. However, those that can also appear after the noun denote partitivity: _es una declaración **cierta**_ 'it is a true statement', to borrow an example from Dozier & Iguina (2017: 41).

  Due to space, and because this chapter is more for teachers and advanced students than for scholars, I will leave it to interested readers to discover for themselves the multiple connections and observations that one can make by "looking inside" (22f). Here are a few. The different order in determiner/ordinal/cardinal (quantifier) in English vis-à-vis Spanish is not a mistake. There is a conjunction between _exciting_ and _interesting_ (in both languages!), but no conjunction between _Spanish_ and _grammar_. The latter are nouns functioning as adjectives. Intuitively, _grammar_ as a type of chapter seems a more natural modifier than _Spanish_ as a type of chapter; hence, _grammar chapter_ should be more frequent than _Spanish chapter_. A "Spanish chapter" in a book should be expressed as the "_chapter in Spanish_". Now it should be clear why _capítulos de gramática del español_ will not raise any eyebrows, but _capítulos del español de la gramática_ will. (It might be possible, but _marked_ – atypical).

## 1.9.  Missed predictions 150 years ago. And now

Bolinger's principle applies to any string of words that makes sense in any language in a particular order. *_Earring golden_ does not make sense in

English, but *golden earring* does. *Special service* makes sense, and so does *service special* (with a difference in meaning), but the probability of two words combining in both orders like *special* and *service* is a special case. Notice that *case special* does not make sense.

Terker (1985: 507) observed that Bolinger's principle of linear modification was at the time the best explanation for adjective position. In his words, "This approach lends itself very nicely to the "direct method", since the explanation is so simple that it can be done at the first-year level completely in Spanish".

Bello (1941[1847]: 12) wrote that the prenominal adjective *"desenvuelve, explica"*, whereas the postnominal adjective *"particulariza, especifica"*, hence the terms explicative and specifying. Robert Ulery (p.c. 2008) observed at a talk that "unfolding" and "explicative" are terms that were already used in Latin grammar to refer to nonrestrictive adjectives. After the 1960s, when scholars began to apply generative grammar to the study of Spanish (Bolinger 1972; Cressey 1969; Luján 1980; Moody 1971; Solé & Solé 1977; Terker 1985; to name only some of those who concerned themselves with adjective position more than 30 years ago), the terms explicative and specifying were replaced with the terms nonrestrictive and restrictive. Those are the terms currently used by many scholars, and crucially by RAE (2009, 2010). However, RAE misses the predictions that those terms make, as §1.4 shows, and as dozens of examples explained incorrectly in RAE (2009, 2010) show.

Bolinger (1972) himself was badly thrown off by adjective position in Spanish. The following is an attempt to extrapolate to Spanish EMPHATIC STRESS in English. Due to word order options, there is no need to raise your voice (or use capitalization in writing in Spanish).

(23) a. *Tenía ricos ORNAMENTOS.*
    'It was richly ornamented'.
  b. *Tenía ornamentos RICOS.*
    'It was ornamented richly'.
  c. *Sufrió terribles DAÑOS.*
    'It was terribly damaged'.
  d. *Sufrió daños TERRIBLES.*
    'It was damaged terribly'.

Presumably, in each phrase, the last word has greater semantic weight. That claim is untenable in Spanish. Perhaps in English as well. In fact, several native speakers of English to whom this author has shown these examples readily realize that (23a,c) are strings in English that listeners will understand right away. However, (23b,d) will raise eyebrows. In Spanish, (23a,c) will be nonrestrictive and (23b,d) will be restrictive. And (23b,d) are well-attested strings in Spanish because they code restrictiveness. Bolinger's word twisting does not suffice in English. English requires adjectival clauses to express the meaning intended in (23b,d): the ornaments, which were rich vs. the ornaments **that were rich**; the damages, which were terrible vs. the damages **that were terrible**. This answers a question that scholars or advanced learners of Spanish might ask themselves: how does English compensate for not having postnominal adjectives? (Except, of course, for a handful of postnominal adjectives borrowed from other languages.)

It is not difficult to challenge the claim that the *right-most* adjective carries "more information". Capitalization in the following examples discussed in Contreras (1978: 47) suggests that the initial element is the one receiving emphasis, which one can assume corresponds with more information:

(24) a.  EMPEZÓ la resistencia.
      began the resistance
      'The resistance began'.
  b.  LA RESISTENCIA empezó.

There is a different explanation, without the need to invoke "emphasis" or "greater importance of an element". *Empezó* is used unaccusatively in (24a) – even if the accusative (the direct object) – is left in situ, since it will require plural agreement if the subject is plural).[17] *La resistencia* is the underlying direct object, and it can be expressed in the canonical position of the direct object in Spanish (right after the verb). However, since there is no subject, the direct object can be "promoted" to the nominative case (the case of the subject), and that explains the order in (24b). Thus, the explanation for (24b) is the same as for passive voice, which is simply "promotion" of the direct object to subject (the underlying direct object is expressed as the subject, when there is not a subject in the sentence). Indeed, passive *se* in Spanish is also unaccusativization, since *se* signals that the grammatical subject is the underlying direct object: *Roberto abrió las puertas, entonces las puertas se abrieron* 'Robert opened the doors, then the doors got opened'. (See Whitley & González (2016, Lesson 7) for a detailed explanation of *se* as unaccusativization – or undativization – for that matter). Incidentally, the sentence in (24) can be expressed not only as in (24a,b); it can also be expressed as *la resistencia se empezó* (passive *se*) and *la resistencia fue empezada* (passive voice).

A similar explanation of contrastive focus (and capitalization in writing) was proposed for the following sentence in Suñer (1982: 236–238).

(25) a.  Surgió PETRÓLEO. (Ex. 81a in Suñer)
      'Oil came-up'.

b. PETRÓLEO surgió. (Ex. 81b in Suñer)
'Oil came-up'.

It turns out that Spanish can show the topicalization of *petróleo* 'oil' with CLEFTING, and without the need for emphatic stress (or capitalization), perhaps an unnecessary calque from English. (*Clefting* is the use of an antecedentless clause – see Chapter 2 – and the verb BE, as in 26a–b). In fact, Suñer (1982: 238) goes on herself to explain that, "The sentences in (81), with their contrastive focused NP, can be readily paraphrased by (87)" [our 26]:

(26) a. *Lo que surgió fue PETRÓLEO.*
'What came-up was oil'. (Ex. 87a in Suñer. Her gloss as well. *Oil* in lower case).
b. PETRÓLEO fue lo que surgió.
'Oil was what came-up'. (Ex. 87b in Suñer. Her gloss as well).

A similar and helpful example for the reader will be (27a,b). Most readers will agree that (27a) is the canonical (typical) order.

(27) a. *Ya llegó el correo.*[18]
already arrived the mail
'The mail arrived already'.
b. *Ya el correo llegó.*

A better understanding of the predictions that restrictiveness makes also explains at least five types of adjectives widely discussed in Spanish and other languages. Are native speakers aware of the categories in §1.9.1 to §1.9.5 below, discussed in Demonte (1999: 137–139)? Or might native speakers be simply computing (non)restrictiveness? More likely the latter, as the evidence adduced in this chapter shows, with the proviso that our understanding has been tainted by an understanding and teaching of (non) restrictiveness with some room for improvement.

### 1.9.1. Descriptive adjectives (calificativos)

Describe a single property of the noun. "Los adjetivos que expresan una sola propiedad son los 'calificativos'", writes Demonte (1999: 137).

(28) *Libro azul, señora delgada, hombre simpático, voz iracunda, frase chillona*
'blue book, slender woman, nice man, furious voice, shrill phrase'

All of the preceding adjectives but one can be used prenominally. Crucially, all of them have a single referent. Those adjectives should be prenominal. Consider these examples:

(29) El simpático entrenador, la dulce voz del entrenador, la iracunda mirada del jugador, la delgada tela de la camiseta, la chillona voz del profesor

### 1.9.2. Relational adjectives (adjetivos relacionales)

Express a set of properties. All of the properties of the corresponding **noun** (Demonte 1999: 137).

(30) puerto **marí**timo, vaca **leche**ra, paseo **cam**pestre
'sea port, milking cow, country walk'

The definition by Bosque 1993 (quoted by Demonte 1999: 138) to explain the examples in (30) appears to be simply *type*. A type is inherently restrictive.[19]

### 1.9.3. Circumstancials (temporals, locative, and manner)

(31) El próximo año, mi antiguo jefe, la última reunión, el reciente atentado, el remoto incidente, el actual intendente, el primer presidente, la cercana casa, la entrada **súbita**, el beso **cortés**, la mirada **dulce**, la furtiva aparición, su sonrisa **benevolente**.

### 1.9.4. Aspectual

(32) El frecuente llamado, las constantes idas y venidas, las periódicas revisiones, la ocasional visita, las reiteradas entradas, las esporádicas crisis, el largo adiós.

(Non)restrictiveness explains all of the adjectives in §1.9.1 to §1.9.4. Including the ones in bold, which can be nonrestrictive in many contexts: la súbita entrada de la decana, el respetuoso/cortés beso del papá, la dulce mirada de la dulce mamá, la benevolente sonrisa de Mr. Rogers.

### 1.9.5. Other adjectives are neither descriptive nor relational.
*They are intensional. The adjective does not apply (or it is possible that it does not apply) to the noun:*

(33) El posible acuerdo, el presunto agresor, el falso amigo, un supuesto asesino (Demonte 1999: 139).

(34) La <u>mera</u> insinuación, la <u>verdadera</u> objeción, una <u>determinada</u> medida, el <u>principal</u> ganador, el <u>único</u> argumento (Demonte 1999: 139).

(Non)restrictiveness explains all of these adjectives as well, without the need for categories that native speakers might not be aware of. Observe also that most of these nouns refer to a single referent in the context in which they are used. Nonrestrictiveness also explains:

(35) a. *el <u>libre</u> albedrío* 'free will'
  b. *la <u>hermosa</u> Dulcinea del Toboso* 'the beautiful Dulcinea del Toboso'
  c. *el <u>nuevo</u> mundo* 'the New World'
  d. *la <u>Santa</u> Misa* 'Holy Mass' (cf. *El viernes **Santo*** 'Good Friday'; la semana **Santa** 'Holy week')
  e. *la <u>Santísima</u> Trinidad* 'the Holy Trinity'
  f. *el <u>Sagrado</u> Corazón de Jesús* 'the Sacred Heart'
  g. *el <u>buen</u> humor de la abuela* 'Grandma's good humor'
  h. *el <u>bendito</u> gato hizo caca en la alfombra* 'the darn cat pooped on the rug'
  i. *la <u>mala</u> suerte del <u>pobre</u> embajador* 'the bad luck of the poor ambassador'

Now it should be clear why people say *la <u>última</u> cena* 'the last supper', *la <u>última</u> cirugía* 'the last surgery', *el <u>último</u> mohicano* 'the last of the Mohicans', *el <u>último</u> suspiro* 'the last breath', *la <u>última</u> noche en París* 'the last night in Paris', *la <u>última</u> palabra* 'the last word', etc. The referent for each of these nouns is an only referent. On the other hand, people say *la recta final de la etapa final* 'the final straight of the final stage'. Ordinarily, there are multiple straight stretches in most road cycling stages. A "one-stage" road-cycling competition is not even called a stage. It is called a one-day race; and the prestigious ones are called *Classics*, with the five most famous among the classics called *Monuments*. (Thanks to Christopher Crafton for these distinctions, p.c. 2019). In fact, *final* is clearly restrictive as applied to virtually any noun. Readers will also understand why the *last* surgery and the *ultimate* surgery (both *la última cirugía* in Spanish) are two very different things. The last surgery will be an autopsy for those who undergo one for legal or medical reasons. Conceivably, an organ transplant for a person is the ultimate surgery in the eyes of their family; but not necessarily the last one.

Now it is also clearer why NAA (noun + adjective + adjective) sequences in Pérez-Leroux et al. (2020) are a mirror image in English (and in other languages), as predicted by increasing restrictiveness to the left in (19) above. Incidentally, relational adjectives (§1.9.2) are not only closer to the noun in Spanish; they are always *immediately postnominal* because they are restrictive. In English, they are immediately prenominal. They are restrictive because they are *type*, which might be a more transparent term than *relational*. In fact, with our definition of *increasing restrictiveness* (our improvement on Bolinger's linear modification) this template must be stated as NA[1]A[2], with A[1] meaning *type* and A[2] meaning *property*. *Type* follows N immediately (to the right or to the left, depending on the language). *Property* can follow or precede N in Spanish if there is no *type*, but it is always on A[1]'s periphery. Nonrestrictiveness predicts that ANA is A[2]NA[1]. It also predicts A[2]N, NA[2], NA[1], and that A[1]N does not occur. NA[2] should not occur if nonrestrictive. It does. §1.10 explains why.

## 1.10. Many nonrestrictive adjectives go after their noun as the result of the omission of *que* + *ser* or *que* + *estar* (copula deletion)

Although it is hard to find a restrictive adjective preceding its noun, plenty of nonrestrictive adjectives follow it, and some of them do so for legitimate reasons. Here are four reasons, the last one being the more interesting one. First, postnominal adjectives might be more frequent than prenominal ones. That issue is left for further research. Second, many textbooks for Spanish as an L2 state that descriptive adjectives follow the noun. That is not true. It will be true to state that *many* descriptive adjectives follow the noun. That is true, simple, and easy enough for beginners to understand. Third, prenominal adjectives in Spanish often have a high-register flair that is believed to evoke a "flowery" or "literary" adornment more than a difference in meaning. That perception is incorrect. It sounds (or reads) more sophisticated because it is correct. Paradoxically, scholars are the ones who have perpetuated that mistake (Bello 1941[1847]; Gili Gaya 1985[1961]; RAE 1973, 2009, 2010; Terker 1985; among many others). The fourth and the really legitimate reason is that a good number of adjectives used nonrestrictively can indeed show up after their noun because they are the result of the omission of *que* + *ser* or *que* + *estar*. Therefore, the adjective that was after *ser* or *estar* remains *in situ* 'in place' after the omission of *que* + *ser* or *que* + *estar*. That omission was called copula deletion when transformational grammar began to be applied to Spanish (Cressey 1969; Luján 1980; among others).

(36) a.  *"Viejo amor" es una famosa canción mexicana.*
      '"An old love" is a famous Mexican song'.
   b.  *"Viejo amor" es una canción* **mexicana** *(que es)* **famosa**.

c. *Ese es un <u>interesante</u> par de frases.*
'That is an interesting pair of phrases'.

d. *Ese es un par de frases* **interesante**. *(= Un par de frases (que es)* **interesante**).

e. *Ayer ocurrió un milagro. Almorzamos en la cafetería de la U y nos sirvieron una <u>deliciosa</u> sopa.*
'A miracle occurred yesterday. We had lunch at the college cafeteria and they served us a delicious soup'.

f. *[…] Nos sirvieron una* **sopa (que estaba)** **deliciosa**.

Here are two examples of a different nature, but that will help readers understand better the omission of *que* + *ser* or *que* + *estar*. It is reasonable to hypothesize that the frequency of the pattern below might be a factor in the use of examples like those above.

(37) a. *Cuando el sujeto es un sustantivo común sin* **modificadores (que es) usado** *antes del verbo, siempre requiere el artículo definido (bajo condiciones normales de acentuación y entonación).*[20]

b. *Algunas de las* **explicaciones [que son] usadas** *en este libro son las mejores del mundo.*
'Some of the explanations used in this book are the best explanations in the world'.

When the past participle does not have a corresponding adjective (*débil* 'weak' is the adjective corresponding to *debilitado/a* 'weakened', *limpio/a* 'clean' is the one for *limpiado/a*, etc.), that past participle must stay in situ. The number of such past participles is *infinite*. Thus, we have an infinite number of past participles requiring postposition. That is a big force at work in a language. The other "force" is the teaching force, to which we owe the incorrect statement that all descriptive adjectives follow the noun.

Therefore, there are at least four very powerful factors to explain why adjective position is still not well understood in Spanish (and in other languages). First, the comprehension of it requires a good comprehension of adjectival clauses, a concept that is restricted to discussions in advanced grammar classes, and therefore unrealistic in a Spanish classroom (Moody 1971). The comprehension of those clauses received a great boost in Spanish after the 1960s, particularly in work by Cressey (1969) and Luján (1980). This proposal owes much to a better comprehension of adjectival clauses, a difficult point of the grammar of any language. Second, there is a strong push of an infinite number of past participial adjectives that must stay after the noun. Third, the repetition of impressionistic observations (a short epithet precedes its noun) that often go without enough scrutiny.

In part, perhaps, because those observations go back to revered scholars, starting with Bello (1941[1847]: 12), who was the first scholar to state the basic distinction in Spanish (explicative/specifying). Fourth, textbooks for Spanish have added their two cents with the statement that adjectives follow the noun in Spanish. Some of those textbooks state that descriptive adjectives follow the noun. Descriptive adjectives can go equally easily before and after. During the months of September and October 2019, two different students told this author that they had learned in Spanish classes before college that *all adjectives* follow the noun in Spanish. The quantifier *all* adds insult to injury. It is well known that quantifying adjectives are prenominal (*all, many, few, several, twenty*, etc.). So are determiners (*the, an, some*). Demonstrative adjectives and possessive adjectives are often prenominal as well. Possessive adjectives can go after the noun when they are new information. As Allie Neal observed (§1.8 above), all of those prenominal words express that the noun + modifier(s) is a totality. Thus, adjectives precede their noun if *adjective + noun* express totality and adjectives follow the noun if *noun + adjective* express part. That is true and it belongs in an elementary L2 textbook. With good examples, many students should understand the distinction without much explanation.

Let us finish this section by making several connections within and outside of this chapter. According to Pérez-Leroux et al. (2020), Sánchez (2017) argues, "that even these rules are too strict; Spanish allows for stacking without ordering, as shown by the possibility of various permutations in (18)". (Our example 38 is example 18 in Pérez-Leroux et al. 2020: 188). Pérez-Leroux et al. (2020: 188) go on to state that there might be differences in preferences by speakers, as Fábregas (2017) had observed. Readers will remember from our discussion of (14a,b) that *red Italian wine* and *Italian red wine* might refer to the same bottle of wine, but only if there is just one bottle of wine in front of us. Something similar is true of a *Peruvian red big bag* or a *Peruvian big red bag*.

(38) a.   Una [[[bolsa roja] grande] peruana]
     b.   Una [[[bolsa roja] peruana] grande]
     c.   Una [[[bolsa grande] roja] peruana]
     d.   Una [[[bolsa grande] peruana] roja]
     e.   Una [[[bolsa peruana] grande] roja]
     f.   Una [[[bolsa peruana] roja] grande]

Leaving aside *Peruvian* for now, it will be a *red big* bag if we have several big bags of different colors. It will be a *big red* bag if we have red bags of different sizes. *Peruvian* should be by world knowledge and by restrictiveness (what we know about *bags, big, Peruvian*, and *red* put together compositionally) the most restrictive modifier in any language. Thus, (38c) and (38a) – in that order – should be more likely than (38b, d–e). (38b) would imply that we have several Peruvian red bags, and only one of them is big. (38d) would imply that we have several Peruvian big bags, and only one of them is red. There might be a little stacking, but it is to represent two different situations in front of our eyes or in front of our mind. Do you see a *Peruvian red big bag* or a *Peruvian big red bag* among other bags? We do not even have to see the bags if (non)restrictiveness is what is at work. With (non)restrictiveness, we can predict how Peruvian red big bags work. Meaning matters. Grammar matters. Readers who would like to test their comprehension can add "paper" as a fourth modifier of this Peruvian red big bag. Paper, as applied to a bag, is more "type" than big (property) or red (property). Type is the closest adjective to the noun, when there is more than one.

## 1.11. Bueno/a, malo/a, serio/a, verdadero/a, último/a, final 'good, bad, serious, true, last, final'

Readers have already seen how *verdadero/a* 'true' works. It is included here because *bueno* and *malo* behave in a similar way. Whitley & González (2016) propose that *bueno/a* preceding a profession or trade refers to competence. Solé & Solé (1977) observed that *bueno/a* and *malo/a* after *hombre* 'man' or *mujer* 'woman' means a person with low ethical standards. Not a good person, morally; a person capable of carrying out bad deeds that will hurt others. Then, an interesting question comes to mind. If a <u>*buen*</u> *abogado* is a competent lawyer; that is, a person competent as a lawyer, would *un buen hombre* and *una buena mujer* be a person (that is) competent as a man or a woman? That begs further scrutiny. Thus, a good lawyer is a competent lawyer and *un hombre malo* is a person capable of bad deeds. Then, *un* <u>*buen*</u> *abogado* can be *un hombre* **malo** and *un* <u>*mal*</u> *abogado* can be *un hombre* **bueno**.

The title of this section was written before this writer ran into *último/a* 'last' and *final* 'final' in the writing of other sections. The only adjective that has not shown up before is *serio/a* 'serious'. A *serio problema* 'a serious problem' and a *verdadero problema* 'a real problem' seem good collocations, but the opposite order is not true for *problema* (*¿problema verdadero?*). If we agree with that, we can also see how speakers might prefer to use the collocation <u>*serio*</u> *problema* vis-à-vis *problema serio*. Noun + *serio/a* is clearly preferred to refer to people: *una mujer* **seria** 'a serious woman', *una estudiante* **seria** 'a serious student'. Along those lines, *un político* **serio** 'a serious politician' makes sense, but *un serio político* does not.[21] However, more than saying the last word, the purpose of this section is an invitation to others to look again at these adjectives from the perspective of (non)restrictiveness. There might be some truth to a difference in meaning in some of the adjectives discussed below, but that difference should be looked at from the system of Spanish, and not simply from a quick and easy translation into English.

### 1.12. Do a few adjectives have one meaning when used before a noun and a different one after it? In part. But it is more totality vs. part

Readers can already predict that a prenominal adjective will be a property of all of the referents to which the noun refers, and that a postnominal adjective will be a property of a part of the referents to which the noun refers. Let us do an example slightly different from the one commonly given in textbooks. And let us have grammatical number give us a hand. The reader will be able to tell the difference between (39a) and (39b):

(39) a.  los <u>altos</u> edificios del distrito comercial de Singapur
        'the tall buildings in Singapur's commercial district'
    b.  los edificios **altos** de Soho en la Ciudad de Nueva York
        'Sojo's tall buildings in New York City'

What is the difference? Restrictiveness. In general, only part of the buildings in Soho, New York, are tall. In general, most people would agree that most of the buildings in Singapur's commercial district are tall.

Now we can see better where the difference lies between *una <u>alta</u> funcionaria* 'a high-ranking officer' and *una empleada **alta*** 'a tall employee'. Dr. Sun Moon can be *una <u>alta</u> funcionaria* 'a high-ranking officer', even if she is 5 ft. tall, if she is the UN Secretary General. On the other hand, if Ms. Jupiter Moon is 6 ft. tall, but she is an intern, she is not *una <u>alta</u> funcionaria*, although she is a *funcionaria **alta***. When speakers refer to Ms. Jupiter Moon as *una funcionaria **alta***, speakers are implicitly comparing her to other people, and according to a standard of comparison, she stands on the taller end of the spectrum. *Alta* 'tall' distinguishes her from other people not as tall as her; *alta* restricts her to part of the employees (or people) with whom speakers compare her. <u>*Alta*</u>, as applied to Dr. Sun Moon as an <u>*alta*</u> *funcionaria*, does not distinguish Dr. Sun Moon from other officers. Saying Dr. Sun Moon and saying a high-ranking officer at the UN is the same.

It will be more accurate to start teaching L2 learners of Spanish (and presumably of other languages with a similar distinction) that *alto/a* before or after the noun is referring to totality if the former; and to part, if the latter. More generally, an adjective before a noun expresses totality. When used after the noun, the same adjective will express partitity. A word like *cierta/o* will have a demonstrative-like or a determiner-like function prenominally (*cierta persona* 'certain person', *cierto tono* 'a certain tone') and a property-like function postnominally (*una respuesta cierta* 'an answer that is true', which clearly sets it apart from other answer(s) that might not be true or correct). If there is a need to avoid an explanation altogether at the elementary level, or during a question in class, *cierta/o* = 'certain' before a noun but *cierto/a* = 'true' after a noun. However, the underlying generalization is that a prenominal adjective is more QUANTIFIER-LIKE, with the understanding that prenominal modifiers tend to *select* a set of referents as a TOTALITY. The corresponding postnominal adjective is more PROPERTY-LIKE, with the understanding that the property selects a PART of the referents of the noun.

We will leave it to the reader to re-think the explanation for many of the pairs of prenominal vs. postnominal adjectives that have a "different meaning": *la rara habilidad* 'the rare ability' vs. *una voz rara* 'a strange voice', *el pobre hombre* 'the unfortunate man' vs. *un hombre pobre* 'a poor man', etc. Dozier & Iguina (2017: 41) have a list of 15 of these pairs. The prenominal ones are nonrestrictive; the postnominal ones, restrictive. With some nuance added by the differences between the two languages, and perhaps by years of explaining these issues somewhat loosely. *Antiguo* 'ancient' in *un antiguo amigo de mi papá* 'a friend of my father's, one with whom he has been friends for a long time' has always struck me as somewhat forced.[22] Would someone refer in any language to a living person as *antiguo/a*; that is, as an 'antique' or 'ancient' person? If a *nuevo coche* 'a different (used) car' is a different car, often not brand new, because a brand new car is a *coche nuevo*, then un *nuevo novio/a* would be a different one, something with which one could agree. However, would *a novio nuevo* be a brand new boyfriend, presumably a newly born baby? That does not add up. Luckily for teachers of Spanish, we can write in teaching materials and say in our classes that what native speakers of Spanish say is that someone has *otro novio* 'another boyfriend' (i.e. a different boyfriend).

**Exercise 5.** Write each phrase or sentence in the best possible order. The words are ordered alphabetically, except for the articles. Sometimes, there are several possible answers. Answers after the exercise.

1. la educativa seria situación del país
2. el aeropuerto bonaerense moderno
3. la caótica, cósmica, violencia
4. un literario movimiento vanguardista
5. la argentina interesante literatura
6. la económica nacional seria situación
7. los ataques continuos partidistas violentos

8. arroz chino frito
9. la familiar preocupante violencia
10. la argentina contemporánea interesante literatura
11. las actuales bélicas estrategias innovadoras
12. una buena noticia verdadera
13. los experimentos nucleares rusos
14. el gobierno militar opresivo
15. la apasionante artística experiencia última
16. la lamentable situación socioeconómica de ese país
17. coreano de español profesor
18. un grupo de hombres racistas

Answers to exercise 5:

1. La educativa seria situación del país. *La seria situación educativa del país*. *Educativa del país* is restrictive as applied to *situación*. Since there is only one *situación educativa del país* at a given time, then *seria* is nonrestrictive as applied to this situation.
2. El aeropuerto bonaerense moderno. *El aeropuerto bonaerense moderno* if there is more than one airport in Buenos Aires, and this one is the modern one. *El moderno aeropuerto bonaerense* if there is only one airport in Buenos Aires.
3. La caótica, cósmica, violencia. *La caótica violencia cósmica*. This example was explained in §1.5.
4. Un literario movimiento vanguardista. *Un movimiento literario vanguardista*. This is an easy one to do with Ngram Viewer (2020): movimiento literario: 0.0000380977%; movimiento vanguardista = 0.0000043612%; movimiento literario vanguardista = 0.0000000672%; movimiento vanguardista literario = 0%.
5. La argentina interesante literatura. *Argentina* is necessarily restrictive as applied to *literatura*. *La literatura argentina interesante* means that only part of it is interesting. *La interesante literatura argentina* means that all of it is interesting.
6. La económica nacional seria situación. *La seria situación económica nacional*. Similar to example number 1.
7. Los ataques continuos partidistas violentos. *Los continuos y violentos ataques partidistas*. *Partidistas* is necessarily restrictive as applied to *ataques*. In view of the polarization in politics in the USA during the Obama administration and the Trump administration, most people would agree that party attacks are all continuous and violent. Hence, the answer proposed. There are other possibilities, but they are not worth mentioning.

8. Arroz chino frito. The reader should be able to tell that *Chinese fried rice* is not the same as *fried Chinese rice*, and that one of them is what is most likely the meaning intended. *Arroz **frito chino*** 'Chinese fried rice' is rice that is fried Chinese style, what one normally orders, under the understanding that said rice does not have to be from China. *Arroz chino frito* 'fried Chinese rice' is rice from China, which is fried (the rice, not China). Whether the rice comes from China is not necessary for it to be *Chinese fried rice*, but *fried Chinese rice* would imply that the rice has to be grown in China.

9. La familiar preocupante violencia. *La preocupante violencia **familiar***. There are several types of violence, hence *violencia familiar*. All *violencia familiar* is concerning.

10. La argentina interesante contemporánea literatura. *La literatura **argentina contemporánea interesante*** means that only part of contemporary Argentinian literature is interesting. *La interesante literatura **argentina contemporánea*** means that all of contemporary Argentinian literature is interesting.

11. Las actuales bélicas estrategias innovadoras. *Las innovadoras estrategias **bélicas actuales***. *Bélicas* is necessarily restrictive as applied to strategies, since there are multiple types of strategies. *Actuales* can further restrict war strategies under the assumption that we are referring to current war strategies. *Innovadoras* can be nonrestrictive under the assumption that all current war strategies are innovating. *Innovadoras* could go after *bélicas* only if some of the war strategies are innovating.

12. Una buena noticia verdadera. *Una verdadera buena noticia*; that is, a good piece of news (a piece of good news) that is really important.

13. Los experimentos nucleares rusos. *Los experimentos **nucleares rusos***. Since there are many types of experiments, it must be *experimentos nucleares*. Since several countries carry out nuclear experiments, *rusos* is necessarily restrictive as applied to *experimentos nucleares* as well. A type of experiment (*nuclear*) is a more natural modifier for the noun *experiment* than *Russian* is a modifier for *experiment*. Therefore, *rusos* is a better further restriction for *experimentos nucleares* than *nucleares* is a further restriction for *experimentos rusos*. (cf. Russian nuclear experiments vs. nuclear Russian experiments).

14. El gobierno militar opresivo. *El opresivo gobierno **militar***. *Militar* is restrictive as applied to a type of government. Since there is ordinarily only one government at a time in a given country, it must be *un opresivo gobierno militar*. The string *gobierno militar opresivo* would imply that there is at least another *gobierno militar* that is not oppressive at the same time in the same country, an unlikely state of affairs.

15. La apasionante experiencia artística última. *Artística* is ordinarily restrictive as applied to *experiencia*. La *última* experiencia **artística** **apasionante**, under the assumption that there was at least another artistic experience that was not riveting. *Última* suggests that there was at least another experience.

16. La lamentable situación socioeconómica de ese país. La *lamentable* situación **socioeconómica** de ese país. *Socioeconómica* is necessarily restrictive as applied to situation of a given country. If there is only one socioeconomic situation at a given moment, that situation would be all regrettable.

17. Coreano de español profesor. A *profesor* **coreano** de español; that is, a professor from Korea who teaches Spanish. A *profesor de español* *coreano* would imply that *Korean Spanish* is a relevant type of Spanish (cf. Argentinian Spanish), a less likely state of affairs than that in which a professor of Spanish is a Korean national. This writer knows well four Korean nationals (two of them born and educated in Korea) who teach Spanish in the USA.

18. Un grupo de hombres racistas. *Un grupo de hombres* **racistas**. The author mentions this example because a student wrote 'un grupo racista de hombres' in a composition. Adjectival clauses and reduction of *que* + *ser* helped in solving the dilemma. The phrase *a group of men who are racists* makes sense whereas *a group of racists who are men* does not make much sense.

## 1.13. Some implications for teaching

The incorrect statement that adjectives follow the noun in Spanish can be easily modified to reflect (non)restrictiveness in terms understood by students: an adjective *precedes* its noun in Spanish when it expresses a property shared by *all of the referents* (people and things) to which the noun refers. An adjective *follows* its noun in Spanish when it expresses a property shared only by **part of the referents** of the noun.

L2 learners of Spanish understand this distinction better when they realize that the same concept is at work in the two main types of adjectival clauses: nonrestrictive and restrictive, a distinction that Chapter 2 explains in more detail. A couple of scholars who read the title of this chapter asked with curiosity why having a *novio* **guapo** might raise some eyebrows. I asked which of the following two sentences they would say or write if they had only one boyfriend: *my boyfriend, who is handsome, is visiting me this weekend* or *my boyfriend, the one who is handsome, is visiting me this weekend.* They immediately conceded that it was the first one, the nonrestrictive one. Even if an L2 learner does not know what nonrestrictive and restrictive adjectival clauses are, most L2 learners will know which of the two sentences referring to someone's boyfriend is the one that native speakers would say, assuming that the person has only one boyfriend. If students can readily understand this difference, the explanation advanced in this chapter belongs in the classroom, and it will be an efficient use of class time. Students do understand it.

## 1.14. Conclusions

A single explanation that an adjective preceding a noun expresses totality and one following it expresses part suffices to account for the four different explanations in Dozier & Iguina (2017: 39) discussed in (6a–d). The same explanation helps to understand why all of the examples from Borges in exercise 2 express totality, and why the adjective precedes the corresponding noun. The same explanation shows why most of the adjectives in exercise 3 must also precede its noun. Totality and partitivity also explain the examples in §1.9.1 to §1.9.5, without the need for the categories discussed in Demonte (1999). Those categories are understood only by scholars. Matthew J. Burner (a doctoral student and teacher of Spanish in college) told this author at a conference where the author presented this explanation in 2020 that it was a great relief to discover that he did not have to keep trying to make sense of those categories. He added that now he does not have to think about how he is going to bring that explanation to the classroom. The totality/part explanation is simpler and sufficient. The fact that an undergraduate student discovered by herself that determiners and quantifiers are nonrestrictive (§1.8) is evidence of how predictive this analysis is. At first sight, understanding why having a *guapo novio* is not going to raise any eyebrows, but having a *novio **guapo*** might do so looks like one more of those quirks that makes learning an L2 challenging and even frustrating. "Unfolding" the meaning – to use the term that some Latin scholars have used to make sense of prenominal adjectives – turns the puzzle into something that L2 learners can easily grasp. The difference in meaning can be unfolded with the perfect paraphrase for an adjective: an adjectival clause. Would you say that *your boyfriend, who is handsome, is visiting you* or would you say that *your boyfriend, the one who is handsome, is visiting you*? The first one, if you have just one boyfriend.

This chapter has explained adjective position in Spanish based on the difference in meaning between nonrestrictive and restrictive adjectival clauses. Chapter 2 explores adjectival clauses in more depth, particularly how the choice of relative pronoun helps in understanding whether the speaker or writer intended a nonrestrictive or a restrictive interpretation.

## Notes

1 A US student who grew up speaking Spanish at home (a heritage speaker of Spanish) told this author at a seminar on Spanish/English grammar when she was a junior in college (2017) that with this example, she understood the distinction for the first time. She had heard and read several explanations before, but had never seen the point.

2 The notation '#' comes from Huddleston & Pullum (2002: 35). It means that the phrase or sentence is semantically anomalous or is not entailed by the sentence at issue.

3 The notation '*' means an ungrammatical sentence. Or better yet, a sentence that native speakers do not use.

4 English has a few adjectives after the noun, but they are borrowings. *Attorney general, inspector general, surgeon general* come from French. *Snow White* comes from the German fairy tale. *Blanca* is a first name in Spanish; *Blanco* is a last name; *Nieves* is a first name.

5 'An adjective specifies the properties or attributes of a noun referent' (SIL 2020).

6 A rule of adjective position in Spanish would read as follows:
  A NONRESTRICTIVE adjective precedes its noun; a RESTRICTIVE adjective follows it.

7 A proper subset is a set whose complement is not the empty set. In simple words, there are other referents of the noun without the property expressed by the adjective.

8 The disambiguation explanation will not help if both nouns have the same gender.

9 Ngrams for *vida nocturna* = 0.0000332518%; *nocturna vida* = 0.0000001480%; *nocturna vida de* = 0. From (Ngram Viewer (2020).

10 Ngram (2000) for '*verdaderamente internacional*': 0.000026638%. (97.54%)
  Ngram (2000) for '*internacional verdadera*': 0.000000663%. From Ngram Viewer (2020)

11 This article came to our attention at the last minute. We were able to read it and confirm that nothing in this chapter needs to be changed. Something similar goes for Cinque (2010), which we could access less than a week before this manuscript was due. Cinque is a much more theoretical study of adjective position and this chapter was already more than 16,000 words long. Furthermore, discussing some of the issues in Cinque vis-à-vis this proposal will require at least a complete article, if not a book. Finally, this presentation is mainly for the teaching of Spanish whereas Cinque is a theoretical study with cross-linguistic scope. Our apologies for not addressing it here. We will be sure to enter the conversation.

12 The author asked Mary Friedman, a specialist on Borges, how she would translate this sentence into English. Within minutes, she came to the author's office with a copy of an anthology by Borges, and read the passage. It reads, "[…] among the effusive honeysuckle vines and the illusory depths of the mirrors" (Borges 1998: 70).

13 In the presence of only one type of wine, the difference can be NEUTRALIZED, a phenomenon that occurs when speakers do not "enforce" a distinction because the meaning is not compromised or ambiguity would not arise. For example, the words in English *pin* and *pen* are pronounced with the same vowel, depending on the dialect. **Indefinite** article + mass noun = **no** article + mass noun = **PP** + mass noun as an object/prepositional object in English:

    i. Borges ate some pie = Borges ate pie = Borges ate at the pie. These three phrases are different from the one in (ii):

    ii. *Borges ate the pie*, which entails that he ate all of his serving (or a whole pie). This in turn entails that there is no pie left (from his serving, or from the whole pie, if that is what he ate).

14 Apparent exceptions are a handful of borrowings (next page), part of speech (crazy rich Asians, discussed in §1.4), and §1.10.

15 Under the assumption that those adjectives are not separated by a comma. In that case, they are nonrestrictive and unordered.

16 'Marked' means atypical; not the default choice. *Attorney General, Inspector General, Surgeon General* are borrowings from French. *Snow White* is a marked string of noun + adjective in English.

17 24a will not be used unaccusatively if both subject (nominative) and object (accusative) are expressed (*los franceses empezaron la resistencia* 'the French began the resistance'). The accusative "unaccusativizes" when it "loses" its accusative case and is expressed as the nominative (the subject).

18 Ngrams for *llegó el correo* = 0.0000015829% (in 2000).
    Ngrams for *el correo llegó* = 0.0000002539% (2,539 is 13.85% of 18,368) (in 2000).
    Ngrams for *llegó el correo* = 0.0000352955% (in 1856).
    Ngrams for *el correo llegó* = 0.0000003403% (3403 is 0,95% of 355,358) (in 1856). From Ngram Viewer (2020).

19 According to Bosque (1993), los adjetivos relacionales son aquellos que "no son calificativos, es decir, […] no denotan cualidades o propiedades de los sustantivos sino […] que establecen conexiones entre esas entidades y otros dominios o ámbitos externos a ellas […]" (relational adjectives are those that "are not descriptive, that is, […] do not denote qualities or properties of their nouns but […] establish connections among those entities and other domains or environments external to them […]" (translation by the author).

20 This is an informal formulation of Suñer's Naked Noun Constraint (Suñer 1982: 209).

21 Ngrams for *un político serio* = 0.0000004243% (in 2000). Ngrams for *un serio político* = 0. (Both searched in November 2019).

22 Dozier & Iguina (2017: 41) do not use *antiguo amigo* (they use *viejo amigo*). They use *antiguo contrato* 'old contract'. Would we really 'teach' *antiguo contrato*? Would one say in English 'antique contract'? Why not *contrato anterior* 'previous contract'? After this author wrote this during final revisions of the manuscript, it occurred to him to check Ngram Viewer (2020). These are the results:
    i. Contrato anterior = 0.0000041620% (2008).
    ii. Anterior contrato = 0.0000019876% (2008).
    iii. Contrato previo = 0.0000031920% (2008).
    iv. Previo contrato = 0.0000015130% (2008).
    v. Contrato anterior = 0.0000386718% (1904).

# References

Bello, Andrés. 1941[1847]. *Gramática de la lengua castellana*. With notes by Rufino J. Cuervo. Buenos Aires: Librería Perlado Editores.

Bolinger, Dwight L. 1952. Linear modification. *PMLA* 67. 1117–1144. (http://www.jstor.com/stable/459963)

Bolinger, Dwight L. 1954. Meaningful word order in Spanish. *Boletín de filología* 8. 45–56.

Bolinger, Dwight L. 1972. Adjective position again. *Hispania* 55. 91–94. (http://www.jstor.com/stable/338250)

Borges, Jorge Luis. 1974. *Obras completas*. Buenos Aires: Emecé Editores.

Borges, Jorge Luis. 1998. *Collected fictions*. New York: Viking. (Translated by Andrew Hurley).

Bull, Wiliam E. 1965. *Spanish for teachers. Applied linguistics*. New York: Ronald Press Company.

Cinque, Guglielmo. 2010. *The syntax of adjectives: A comparative study*. (Linguistic Inquiry Monographs 57). Cambridge: MIT Press. (https://doi.org/10.7551/mitpress/9780262014168.001.0001)

Contreras, Heles. 1978. *El orden de palabras en español*. Madrid: Cátedra.

Cressey, William. 1969. Teaching the position of Spanish adjectives: A transformational approach. *Hispania* 52. 878–881. (https://www.jstor.org/stable/337652)

Demonte, Violeta. 1999. El adjetivo: Clases y usos. La posición del adjetivo en el sintagma nominal. In Bosque, Ignacio & Demonte, Violeta (eds.), *Gramática descriptiva de la lengua española*, vol. 1, 129–215. Madrid: Espasa Calpe S.A.

Dozier, Eleanor & Iguina, Zulma. 2017. Manual de gramática. *Grammar reference for students of Spanish*, 6th ed. Boston: Cengage Learning. (Instructor's edition).

Fábregas, Antonio. 2017. The syntax and semantics of nominal modifiers: Interpretation, types, and ordering facts. *Borealis: An International Journal of Hispanic Linguistics* 6. 1–102. (https://doi.org/10.7557/1.6.2.4191)

Gili Gaya, Samuel. 1985[1961]. *Curso superior de sintaxis española*. 15th reprint. Barcelona: Biblograf.

Huddleston, Rodney & Pullum, Geoffrey K. 2002. *The Cambridge grammar of the English language*. Cambridge: Cambridge University Press. (https://www.cambridge.org/9780521431460)

Kwan, Kevin. 2013. *Crazy rich Asians*. New York: Random House, Inc.

Kwan, Kevin. 2018. *Locos, ricos y asiáticos*. Barcelona: Editorial Suma de letras (A division of Penguin Random House). (Translated by Jesús de la Torre).

Luján, Marta. 1980. *Sintaxis y semántica del adjetivo*. Madrid: Cátedra.

Marín, Rafael. 2016. Ser y estar. In J. Gutiérrez-Rexach (Ed.), *Enciclopedia de lingüística hispana*, vol. 2, 13–24. London: Routledge.

Moody, Raymond. 1971. More on teaching Spanish adjective position: Some theoretical and practical considerations. *Hispania* 54. 315–321. (https://www.jstor.org/stable/337791)

Ngram Viewer. 2020. (https://books.google.com/ngrams)

Ozete, Óscar. 1981. Current usage of adjectival pronouns in Spanish. *Hispania* 64. 85–91.

Pérez-Leroux, Ana T., Tough, Alexander, Pettibone, Erin , & Chen, Crystal. 2020. Restrictions on ordering of adjectives in Spanish. *Borealis: An International*

*Journal of Hispanic Linguistics* 9(1). 181–208. (https://dx.doi.org/10.7557/1.9 .1.5277)

RAE (Real Academia Española). 1973. *Esbozo de una nueva gramática de la lengua española*. Madrid: Espasa Calpe S.A.

RAE (Real Academia Española y Asociación de Academias de la Lengua Española). 2009. *Nueva gramática de la lengua española. Morfología y sintaxis I*. Madrid: Espasa Libros S.L. (https://www.rae.es/obras-academicas/gramatica/nueva-gra matica)

RAE (Real Academia Española y Asociación de Academias de la Lengua Española). 2010. *Nueva gramática de la lengua española. Manual*. Madrid: Espasa Libros S.L.U. (https://www.rae.es/obras-academicas/gramatica/manual-de-la-nueva-gramatica)

Sagan, Carl. 1995. *The demon-haunted world: Science as a candle in the dark*. New York: Penguin Random House, LLC.

Sánchez, Liliana. (2017). Adjetivos atributivos postnominales y estructuras predicativas. (Paper presented at the 48th Linguistics Symposium on Romance Languages. Toronto: York University).

SIL (Summer Institute of Linguistics). 2020. *Glossary of linguistic terms*. (https://gl ossary.sil.org/term/stative-verb) (Last accessed 2020)

Solé, Yolanda & Solé, Carlos. 1977. *Modern Spanish syntax*. Lexington: DC Heath.

Stockwell, Robert P. & Bowen, J. Donald & Martin, John W. 1965. *The grammatical structures of English and Spanish*. Chicago: University of Chicago Press.

Suñer, Margarita. 1982. *Syntax and semantics of Spanish presentational sentence-types*. Washington: Georgetown University Press.

Terker, Andrew. 1985. On Spanish adjective position. *Hispania* 68. 502–509. (https://www.jstor.org/stable/342445)

Thompson, Michael. 2020. *La posición de los adjetivos*. (http://www.dur.ac.uk/m.p. thompson/adjectives.htm) (Last accessed 2020)

Thought Company. 2020. (https://www.thoughtco.com/felicity-conditions-speech -1690855) (Last accessed 2020)

Whitley, M. Stanley. 2002. *Spanish/English contrasts. A course in Spanish linguistics*, 2nd ed. Washington: Georgetown University Press. (http://press.ge orgetown.edu/book/languages/spanishenglish-contrasts)

Whitley, M. Stanley & González, Luis. 2016. *Gramática para la composición*, 3rd ed. Washington: Georgetown University Press. (http://press.georgetown.edu/bo ok/languages/gramática-para-la-composición-0)

# 2    Whole/part matters

## Nonrestrictive and restrictive adjectival (relative) clauses

*Luis H. González*

## 2.1. Introduction

This chapter shows that choosing the best relative pronoun is much easier with a better understanding of nonrestrictive and restrictive adjectival clauses. Nonrestrictiveness and restrictiveness is a distinction often ignored when textbooks explain the choice of relative pronoun without using it, and without using the differences in punctuation (comma) that often go hand-in-hand with these two types of adjectival clauses. This chapter explains the difference between nonrestrictive and restrictive adjectival clauses using examples written mostly by L2 learners of Spanish in their compositions in college. The distinction between nonrestrictivity and restrictivity is easily internalized because when learners see a nonrestrictive and a restrictive adjectival clause contrasted, they can readily understand the difference in meaning, even if they have never heard the terms (non)restrictive. This chapter also uses examples from RAE (2010) and from readings from the Centro Virtual Cervantes (https://cvc.cervantes.es). Section 2 explains the difference between nonrestrictive adjectival clauses; that is, clauses that refer to all of the referents expressed by the antecedent (the noun that the adjectival clause modifies) and restrictive adjectival clauses; that is, clauses that refer to a part of the referents expressed by the antecedent. Section 3 is a table that shows how to choose the most informative relative pronoun; that is, the relative pronoun that helps the listener/reader understand more easily whether the adjectival clause is nonrestrictive or restrictive. It shows that the series *article* + *cual/cuales* is the nonrestrictive series whereas the series (*article*) + *que* is the restrictive one. It also shows when *que*, the "generic" relative is mandatory and when *article* + *cual/cuales* or *quien/quienes* is preferable. That table is in a section by itself with examples numbered from 1 to 15. Section 4 adds a few observations to Table 2.3. It also adds to the evidence that the difference between *article* + *cual/cuales* and *article* + *que* is not a matter of disambiguation, prosody, or higher register, as commonly stated in textbooks and in some scholarly accounts. Forms of *article + cual(es)* code nonrestrictivity; forms of *article + que* code restrictivity. Section 5 adds evidence from antecedentless relative clauses and from clauses whose antecedent is an entire sentence that the relative *lo que* 'what' is restrictive and *lo cual* 'which' is nonrestrictive. This section also expands the explanation in Table 2.3 and in section 4 on why a relative pronoun different from the "generic" *que* is often preferred and sometimes mandatory. Adjectival clauses headed by a prepositional phrase (e.g. we carefully chose the exercises *with which we practice relative pronouns*) get the special attention and extra practice that they deserve. Finally, dozens of exercises (with answers provided) will help learners to distinguish nonrestrictive adjectival clauses from restrictive ones, choose the sentence with the relative pronoun that shows best the distinction, and put together two sentences by modifying an antecedent in the main clause with an adjectival clause. Section 6 suggests some implications for teaching. Section 7 offers conclusions.

Note: Specialized or key terms are capitalized when introduced. They are explained or exemplified as needed.

## 2.2. Nonrestrictive and restrictive adjectival clauses

Observe sentences (1a,b) and (1d,e), and how the repetition of a common noun in sentences (1a,b) and (1d,e) (*boyfriend* and *tool*) is avoided by combining (1a,b) as in (1c) and (1d,e) as in (1f). The mention of a noun a second time is avoided by replacing it with an appropriate RELATIVE PRONOUN (*who* and *that* in this case):

(1)   a.   My boyfriend[1] is visiting me this weekend.
       b.   My boyfriend[2] is handsome.
       c.   My boyfriend[1], who[2] is handosme, is visiting me this weekend.
       d.   A hammer is a tool[1].
       e.   A tool[2] is used to drive nails.
       f.   A hammer is a tool[1] **that[2] is used to drive nails**.
       g.   A hammer is a tool[1] used to drive nails.

The noun that is not repeated in (1c,f) is called the ANTECEDENT of an adjectival clause. The ANTECEDENT is the noun that an ADJECTIVAL CLAUSE modifies. The sentences in (1a) and (1d) are called the main (or matrix) sentence. The sentences in (1b) and (1e) (when they are embedded in 1c,f) are called an ADJECTIVAL CLAUSE because they function as an adjective that modifies the *antecedent* (my handsome *boyfriend* and a **nail-driving** *tool*). Observe also that (1b) "stands" on its own, but (1e) seems an incomplete sentence. It is too vague, and it would imply that the only tool is a nail-driving one. Likewise, (1d) is somewhat vague and requires narrowing down to be easily interpretable. The string of words *who is handsome* in (1c) is called a <u>NONRESTRICTIVE</u> ADJECTIVAL CLAUSE and the string *that is used to drive nails* in (1f) is called a **RESTRICTIVE** ADJECTIVAL CLAUSE. A nonrestrictive adjectival clause expresses a property shared by <u>all</u> of the REFERENTS to which the antecedent refers. A restrictive adjectival clause expresses a property of **PART** of the REFERENTS to which the antecedent refers. REFERENT(S) is the people or thing(s) in the world to which a noun refers. If you are reading a paper version of this book, the referent for *book* is the object that you are reading right now. Finally, the sentence in (1f) can be "reduced" to (1g) by omitting the relative pronoun (*that*) and the verb *be*, an omission commonly called COPULA DELETION (Cressey 1969; Luján 1980; among others). The name comes from the fact that the verb *be* is the prototypical copular verb in the languages of the world with copular verbs.[1]

Let us now call attention again (as in Chapter 1) to the connection between adjectival clauses and adjectives in Spanish. Many adjectives can go before the noun (prenominally) or after the noun (postnominally). We will make that connection by briefly explaining from a different angle the title of the first chapter of this book: why having a *guapo novio* (a boyfriend, who is handsome) does not raise any eyebrows, but having a *novio* **guapo** (one boyfriend that is handsome) might. Observe that *guapo* 'handsome' precedes *boyfriend* 'novio' in the first part of the sentence, but follows it in the second part. <u>Spanish (and other</u> languages) code a difference <u>in meaning by the position of some adjectives before or after its noun.</u>[2] The difference in meaning is the same that one can see in the following two sentences:

(2)  a.  My boyfriend, <u>who is handsome</u>, is visiting me this week.[3]
     b.  My boyfriend, **the one who is handsome**, is visiting me this week.

Sentence (2a) means that you have one boyfriend, and that said boyfriend is handsome. Sentence (2b) means that you have more than one boyfriend. The adjectival clause in sentence (2a) – who is handsome – is a NONRESTRICTIVE adjectival clause. A nonrestrictive adjectival clause offers information not needed to understand the main sentence (my boyfriend is visiting me this weekend). Most nonrestrictive adjectival clauses are set off within commas – or preceded by a comma if they come at the end of the sentence. Furthermore, they can be left out of the sentence without changing the meaning of the main sentence (without changing its truth-value). Observe that the information *my boyfriend is handsome* in (3a), if added to (3b), does not change its truth-value: if (3b) is true without (3a), it will also be true with it.

(3)  a.  My boyfriend is handsome.
    b.  My boyfriend is visiting me this week.

On the other hand, the adjectival clause in sentence (2b) – **the one who is handsome** – is a RESTRICTIVE adjectival clause. A restrictive adjectival clause is needed to restrict – limit the extent of – the meaning of the ANTECEDENT. That is, a restrictive clause refers to a part of the people or things denoted by the antecedent. The antecedent in sentence (1c) is *boyfriend* and in (1f) is *tool*. Consider now (4b), the latter being sentence (4a) without its restrictive adjectival clause (*that produce ebooks*). The antecedent in (4a) is *publishers*:

(4)  a.  Publishers **that produce ebooks** have a competitive advantage.
    b.  Publishers have a competitive advantage.

Observe that sentence (4b) does not make sense without the restrictive adjectival clause (that produce ebooks). Sentence (4b) means that all publishers have a competitive advantage, which is irrelevant because if all of them have a competitive advantage, none of them has it, really. Sentence (4b) is incomplete without specifying a type of publishers from all publishers. Consider (5), repeated from Chapter 1:

(5)  They sent them the important information.

Sentence (5) has two different interpretations. Those two interpretations are difficult to see with just the adjective *important*. However, if we "unfold" the sentence using adjectival clauses, the difference jumps out:[4]

(6)  a.  They sent them the information, *which is important*.
    b.  They sent them the information *that is important*.

The reader will remember now the difference in meaning. Sentence (6a) means that all of the information is important. The adjectival clause *which is important* is nonrestrictive. It describes all of the information as important. Sentence (6b) is restrictive. It distinguishes the information that is important from the part that is not. Only the important part was sent. The sentences in (6) answer an important question: how does English (and other languages) do without having postnominal adjectives (except for a few borrowings)? If there is a need to code the difference in meaning in (6a–b), English will require the use of an adjectival clause. Observe the difference in relative pronoun and in punctuation.

To state it in slightly different terms, a restrictive adjectival clause restricts (e.g. limits) the meaning of its antecedent, and indicates that the property expressed by it applies only to a part of the referents of the antecedent. It distinguishes a subset of the nouns that have that property from other part of the referents of the noun that does not have it. A nonrestrictive adjectival clause states a property shared by all of the referents of the noun that the adjectival clause modifies.

Let us summarize our discussion until now with the definition of **restrictive** (specifying) and <u>nonrestrictive</u> (explicative) adjectival clauses in RAE (2010: 838). According to RAE, specifying or restrictive sentences:

> [...] precisan la denotación del grupo nominal del que forman parte [...]. Las explicativas agregan, en cambio, cierta información, pero no restringen la denotación del grupo nominal: en el ejemplo mencionado con oración explicativa se entiende que todos los documentos serán fundamentales y que todos los documentos se salvaron del incendio.
>
> [...] determine the denotation of the nominal group of which they are a part [...]. The explicative ones add, instead, certain information, but they do no restrict the denotation of the nominal group: in the example mentioned with the explicative sentence, it is understood that all of the documents will be essential and that all of them were saved from burning. (Translation by the author).

The examples to which RAE refers are *los documentos que se salvaron del incendio serán fundamentales en el juicio* 'the documents that were saved from the fire will be essential in the court case' (restrictive) and *los documentos, que se salvaron del incendio, serán fundamentales en el juicio* 'the documents, that were saved from the fire, will be essential in the court case'.

**Exercise 1.** Now readers can confirm their understanding by doing the following exercise. The equivalent exercise in English follows the one in Spanish. The task is to determine which of each pair of sentences makes sense in the world in which we live. It is possible that in a few cases both sentences make sense, but with a difference in meaning. The point of the exercise is whether the adjectival clause in italics expresses a property of <u>all of the referents</u> denoted by the noun – including an only referent when all of the referents is a single referent – or whether the adjectival clause distinguishes *a part of the referents* with that property from other referents that do not share that property. Readers can refer to Table 2.3 to understand better why the relative pronoun (and sometimes the punctuation) is different in the sentences on the left from those on the right. See Tables 2.1 and 2.2

**Answers to exercise 1.** Sentence (1a) is nonrestrictive. It means that there is only one President of ACTFL, and that she is an outstanding

*Table 2.1* Exercise 1 in Spanish

| | |
|---|---|
| 1a La Presidenta de ACTFL, <u>quien es una profesora sobresaliente</u>, dará el discurso plenario. | 1b La Presidenta de ACTFL, **la que es una profesora sobresaliente**, dará el discurso plenario. |
| 2a El Dr. Fingercut, <u>quien vive al lado</u>, se ganó un premio a nivel nacional este mes. | 2b El Dr. Fingercut, **el que vive al lado**, se ganó un premio a nivel nacional este mes. |
| 3a Los jugadores, <u>quienes se habían duchado</u>, pudieron participar todos en la rueda de prensa. | 3b Los jugadores **que se habían duchado** pudieron participar en la rueda de prensa. |
| 4a A la directora del hospital, <u>quien estaba de vacaciones</u>, la operaron de urgencia. | 4b A la directora del hospital que estaba de vacaciones la operaron de urgencia. |
| 5a El calor de julio en Miami, <u>el cual es intenso</u>, calienta la arena un poco más de la cuenta. | 5b El calor de julio en Miami, **el que es intenso**, calienta la arena un poco más de la cuenta. |

*Table 2.2* Exercise 1 in English

| | |
|---|---|
| 1a The President of ACTFL, <u>who is an outstanding teacher</u>, will give the keynote speech. | 1b The President of ACTFL, **the one who is an outstanding teacher**, will give the keynote speech. |
| 2a Dr. Fingercut, <u>who lives next door</u>, won a national award this month. | 2b Dr. Fingercut, **the one who lives next door**, won a national award this month. |
| 3a The players, <u>who had taken a shower</u>, could all participate in the press conference. | 3b The players that **had taken a shower** could participate in the press conference. |
| 4a The director of the hospital, <u>who was on vacation</u>, had an emergency procedure. | 4b The director of the hospital **who was on vacation** had an emergency procedure. |
| 5a The heat in July in Miami, <u>which is intense</u>, warms the sand a bit too much. | 5b The heat in July in Miami, **the one that is intense**, warms the sand a bit too much. |

teacher. Sentence (1b) is restrictive. It means that there are at least two presidents of ACTFL, and that only one is an outstanding teacher. Sentence (1a) expresses a situation more likely to occur than (1b). Sentence (2a) is nonrestrictive. It means that we know a doctor whose last name is Fingercut, that he lives next door, and that he won a national award this month. Sentence (2b) is restrictive. It means that we know at least two doctors whose last name is Fingercut, and that only one of them lives next door. Sentence (2a) expresses a situation more likely to occur than (2b). Sentence (3a) is nonrestrictive. It means that all of the players had showered, and that all of them were able to participate in the press conference. Sentence (3b) is restrictive. It means that only some of the players had showered, and only those were able to participate in the press conference.

It is a common practice that only a few members of a sport team participate in a press conference. Sentence (3b) expresses a situation more likely to occur than (3a). Sentence (4a) is nonrestrictive. It means that there is only one director of the hospital, that she was on vacation, and that she had an emergency procedure. Sentence (4b) is restrictive. It means that there are at least two directors of the hospital and that one of them was on vacation and had an emergency procedure. When there is more than one director in any institution, that state of affairs is often indicated with a modifier: the director of finances, the director of operations, etc. Sentence (4a) is more likely than (4b). Sentence (5a) is nonrestrictive. It means that the heat in Miami is intense every day in July, and that it warms the sand a bit too much. Sentence (5b) is restrictive. It means that there are different "heats" in Miami, but that only one is intense in July, and that it warms the sand a bit too much. What (5b) would actually mean is that the heat is not intense every day in July in Miami.

This section has explained nonrestrictive and restrictive adjectival clauses using examples, has shown the important difference in meaning that they express, and has given readers an opportunity to test their comprehension by completing an exercise in Spanish and its equivalent in English.

## 2.3. Choosing the best (most informative) relative pronoun

Table 2.3 summarizes the choice of relative pronoun. "Most informative" means that the relative pronoun helps the listener/reader to understand more easily the intended nonrestrictive or restrictive interpretation. Or grasp the real difference in meaning in sentences with an antecedent modified by a prepositional phrase (sentences 5 and 7 in Table 2.3 and also sentences 10 and 11 in §2.4). A few additional observations and examples follow Table 2.3. Those observations and examples will help readers in choosing the best relative pronoun.

Translation of the examples in Table 2.3 (most of them not translated in the table):

(1)  Joseph, who was the director, is now the Chief Operations Officer.
(2)  The woman with whom they spoke is the captain of the team.
(3)  We went to the restaurant that you recommended to me.
(4)  Yesterday, we saw the student who did not go to the party.
(5)  Hillary's daughter, *who/\*the one who* is supersmart, spoke in defense of Barron Trump.
(6)  *Which leaves last, turns the lights off.[6]
(7)  B. Bush's son, *\*who/the one who* was the Governor of Texas, was also President of the USA.

*Table 2.3* Choosing the best (most informative) relative pronoun (Examples are translated below the table)

| NONRESTRICTIVE RELATIVE PRONOUNS | RESTRICTIVE RELATIVE PRONOUNS |
|---|---|
| QUIEN (= who) PREFERRED when the ANTECEDENT is [+human], except in RESTRICTIVE adjectival clauses whose antecedent is not followed by a preposition.[5] <br> (1) *JOSÉ, quien era el director, es ahora el jefe de operaciones.* <br> (2) *La MUJER con quien hablaron es la capitana del equipo. (Quien* is used in nonrestrictive as well as in **restrictive** clauses.) | QUE (= that) MANDATORY in a RESTRICTIVE CLAUSE when nothing intervenes between the ANTECEDENT and the relative pronoun, regardless of whether the ANTECEDENT is [+human] or [-human]: <br> (3) *Fuimos al RESTAURANTE que me recomendaste.* <br> (4) *Ayer vi al ESTUDIANTE que no fue a la fiesta.* |
| EL CUAL (= which/who) (El/la/los/las CUAL/ES) Used when something intervenes between the ANTECEDENT and the relative pronoun: <br> (5) *La HIJA de Hillary, la cual/\*la que es superinteligente, salió a la defensa de Barron Trump.* <br> CANNOT be used in antecedentless ("headless") adjectival clauses (clauses whose antecedent is not explicit) because headless adjectival clauses are always restrictive. <br> (6) *\*El cual salga de último, apaga las luces.* | EL QUE (= the one that) (El/la/los/las/QUE) Used when something intervenes (usually Prep + Noun) between the ANTECEDENT and the relative pronoun: <br> (7) *El HIJO de B. Bush, el que/\*el cual fue gobernador de Texas, fue Presidente de Estados Unidos.* <br> Used in headless adjectival clauses whose antecedent is [+human]. QUIEN(ES) is preferred because it encompasses both genders: <br> (8) *Quien salga de último/a, apaga las luces.* <br> (9) *El que salga de último/a, apaga las luces.* |
| LO CUAL (= which, who) The ANTECEDENT for LO CUAL is not a noun, but the whole sentence. <br> (10) *MI CUARTO ESTÁ EN LA ESQUINA DEL EDIFICIO, lo cual significa que tengo dos vistas distintas desde la ventana.* (Ex. written by a student in college.) <br> (11) *NO REGRESARON, lo cual nos preocupa.* (Ex. From Ozete (1981: 90.) although he wrote it as, "No regresaron, lo que (cual) nos preocupa".) | LO QUE (= what) USED in headless adjectival clauses. The gender and number of the implicit ANTECEDENT of a headless adjectival clause is underspecified or unknown (= the thing that/the things that). <br> (12) *Lo que necesitas es muy distinto de lo que quieres.* <br> (13) *Lo que me dijiste no tiene sentido.* <br> (14) *Lo que está escrito en este libro siempre se apoya con ejemplos.* |

*(Continued)*

*Table 2.3* (Continued)

| NONRESTRICTIVE RELATIVE PRONOUNS | RESTRICTIVE RELATIVE PRONOUNS |
|---|---|
| | **CUYA/ CUYO/ CUYAS/ CUYOS (= whose)** It is the possessive (adjectival) relative pronoun. It goes between the ANTECEDENT and the <u>noun possessed</u>, and it agrees with the latter. (15) *Los ESTUDIANTES **cuyas** <u>tarjetas</u> no hayan sido renovadas deben hacerlas renovar inmediatamente.* |

(8) **She/he who** leaves last, turns the lights off.

(9) **The one who** leaves last, turns the lights off. (The last one to leave, turns the lights off).

(10) My room is in the corner of the building, *\*that/<u>which</u>* means that I have two different views from my window.

(11) They did not return, <u>which</u> worries us.

(12) **What** you need is very different from **what** you want.

(13) **What** you told me does not make sense.

(14) **What** is written in this book is always supported with examples.

(15) Those students **whose** cards have not been renewed should have them renewed immediately.

## 2.4. A few additional observations on the choice of relative pronoun

First, **QUIEN** is preferred over **EL QUE (LA QUE/LOS QUE/LAS QUE)** in antecedentless adjectival clauses to refer to people. Observe that *quien(es)* expresses with one word *las personas que/las que/los que/aquellas que/aquellos que, la gente que,* and even *aquellas quienes/aquellos quienes. Quien* can be used in nonrestrictive or in restrictive adjectival clauses.

(7) ***Quien** ríe de último, ríe mejor.*
      'He/she who laughs last, last better'.

Second, although QUE can be used with a [+human] ANTECEDENT in <u>NONRESTRICTIVE</u> clauses, QUIEN(ES) is preferred in writing. If there is a preposition, QUIEN(ES) is highly preferable. The presence of a preposition after a [+human] antecedent is such a powerful trigger for QUIEN(ES) that the adjectival clause can be nonrestrictive or restrictive (see sentences 1 and 2 in Table 2.3).

Third, the pronoun **QUE** can be used after four prepositions (*a, con, de, en*). However, after ANY preposition (including these four), EL CUAL/**EL QUE** are preferred over QUE.[7] (See sentence 11 below)

Fourth, after ALL prepositions, EL CUAL is preferred (over **EL QUE**) because most of these clauses are nonrestrictive, NOT because EL CUAL is required for prosodic reasons, as claimed in RAE (2010: 843) or for stylistic reasons (a higher register) as claimed by Gili Gaya (1985[1961]) and others.

(8) *Tú eres una de las estudiantes <u>sin las cuales</u>/ %**sin las que** no sabríamos si estas reglas funcionan.*
'You are one of the students <u>without whom</u>/*without that* we would not know whether these rules work'.

(9) *Se oye mucho ruido en los edificios <u>detrás de los cuales</u>/ %**de los que** hay construcción.*
'A lot of noise can be heard in the buildings <u>behind which</u>/*behind that* there is construction'.

Fifth, as Whitley (2002: 277) observes, many textbooks state that when the gender of two possible "antecedents" is different (as in *compartía un apartamento con el hijo de Gloria, el cual vivía en Bello* in 10 below), the article "helps" in determining to which of the two antecedents the adjectival clause refers. Only the first of the two nouns is the antecedent (*el hijo*); *de Gloria* is a modifier of *el hijo*. The adjectival clause *cannot* refer to the modifier; therefore, there is never a need to disambiguate. The difference between <u>el cual</u>/**el que** is that the former refers to the totality of the referents of the antecedent (Gloria has one son), whereas the latter refers to a subset of the referents (Gloria has at least two sons). Ozete (1981: 91) reports that, "eleven of the fifteen texts examined mention the use of *el que (cual)* for purposes of clarifying the antecedent".

(10) *Compartía un apartamento con el HIJO de Gloria, <u>el cual</u> vivía en Bello.*
'She/he shared an apartment with Gloria's son, who lived in Bello'.
(Implies that Gloria has only one son.)

(11) *La HIJA de Gloria, <u>la cual</u>/**la que** vive en Sabaneta, nos trajo fotos de la iglesia.*
'Gloria's daughter, <u>who</u>/**the one who** lives in Sabaneta, brought us pictures of the church'.

*La cual*: Gloria has only one daughter.
*La que*: Gloria has at least two daughters.

## 2.5.  Relative pronouns: why settle for the generic *que* 'that' when you can choose a relative pronoun that helps your listener/reader?

There is room for improvement in the explanation for relative pronouns in many textbooks. For example, a reputable reference grammar for Spanish explains relative pronouns by just providing a translation into English of each example. The seven-page explanation does not mention a single time (non)restrictivity nor does it call attention to the difference in punctuation. Many teachers (and perhaps many students) who understand the main points in Table 2.3 would change some of the relative pronouns in the examples in that reference grammar.

Although pedagogical grammars often suggest that speakers can choose between two or three relative pronouns (Butt & Benjamin 1988: 378; DeMello 1993: 93; Dozier & Iguina 2017: 93–95; Lunn & DeCesaris 2007: 142–144; Ozete 1981: 90; Whitley & González 2016: 307; among others), those putative choices reflect an incomplete understanding of (non)restrictivity. The difference between *lo cual* vs. *lo que* offers an uncontroversial clue as to the distinction. As §1.10 in Chapter 1 showed, nonrestrictive modifiers can be used instead of restrictive ones ("Viejo amor" es una <u>famosa</u> canción de México vs. *"Viejo amor" es* una canción **famosa** de México), but a restrictive modifier is virtually never used instead of a nonrestrictive one (los novelistas **mexicanos** vs. *los mexicanos novelistas). Thus, *lo que* is commonly used instead of *lo cual*, (as in the first part of 12a below), but *lo cual* can never be used instead of *lo que* in sentences similar to the second part of that same sentence. In fact, in antecedentless adjectival clauses, as in (12b), *lo cual* is impossible, and no native speaker says or writes sentences like (12c).

(12) a.   Uno puede identificarse con la película porque discutía los proble-mas de asistir a la universidad, <u>lo cual</u>/%**lo que** es exactamente <u>lo que</u>/*lo cual ocurría en la vida de los jóvenes que vieron *Toy Story 1* cuando eran niños.
'One can relate with the movie because it discussed the problems of attending college, which/*what is exactly what/*which was occurring in the life of the young people who saw *Toy Story 1* when they were children'.

   b.   **Lo que** está escrito en este libro es el resultado de miles de horas de trabajo.
'What is written in this book is the result of thousands of hours of work'.

   c.   \*<u>Lo cual</u> está escrito en este libro es el resultado de miles de horas de trabajo.

'\*Which is written in this book is the result of thousands of hours of work'.

Observe that (12c) is ungrammatical both in Spanish and in English. Observe also the use of *lo cual* in (12a) as the antecedent for the whole sentence. Although *lo que* is common in Spanish, it is a failure to distinguish between antecedentless relative clauses (as in the second part of 12a and in 12b), which are always RESTRICTIVE, and adjectival clauses whose antecedent is the whole sentence (as in the first part of 12a), which are always NONRESTRICTIVE. Speakers often use *lo que* istead of *lo cual* in their speech in sentences similar to the first part of (12a), but many writers – and some speakers – have the intuition that *lo cual* is better, although many of those writers are not explicitly aware of the reason. Interestingly, *lo que* is mandatory as the antecedentless adjectival clause in the second part of the sentence. Notice that neither can *lo cual* be used in Spanish nor can *which* be used in English. Whole and part matters. Most writers (and some speakers) will notice the repetition if they produce *lo que* twice in sentences similar to (12a). Many of them will change one to *lo cual*, and it will invariably be the first one. The wisdom of language. More importantly, uncontroversial evidence which shows that *article* + *cual/cuales* is the nonrestrictive relative pronoun and *(article)* + *que* is the restrictive relative pronoun.

Let us turn to (13a–f) in order to point out that the use of *quien(es)* in (13d) is a better choice than *los* + *noun* + *que* (13c), which in theory can refer to a mix of masculine and feminine referents.

(13) a.  Los niños que vieron *Toy Story 1* asistieron a la universidad unos diez años después.

'Children who watched *Toy Story 1* went to college about ten years later'.

     b.  Las niñas que vieron *Toy Story 1* asistieron a la universidad unos diez años después.

'Girls who watched *Toy Story 1* went to college about ten years later'.

     c.  Los que vieron *Toy Story 1* asistieron a la universidad unos diez años después.

'Those who watched […]'

     d.  Quienes vieron *Toy Story 1* asistieron a la universidad unos diez años después.

'Those who watched […]'

    e.  *Los cuales vieron *Toy Story 1* asistieron a la universidad unos diez años después.
       '*Those which watched *Toy Story 1* went to college about ten years later'.
    f.  *Las cuales vieron *Toy Story 1* asistieron a la universidad unos diez años después.

It is conceivable that in most contexts, *los* + *noun* + *que* comprises *las* + *noun* + *que*. However, the use of *quienes* (as in 13d) is preferred because it clearly encompasses both *las que* and *los que* as well as *las cuales* and *los cuales* (the latter not in sentences like 13, of course). Sentences (13e,f) prove that (13c,d), by virtue of being antecedentless, are restrictive. Therefore, the nonrestrictive sentences (13e,f) are impossible. Sentences (13e,f) also add to the evidence that the relative QUIEN can be used in restrictive and nonrestrictive relative clauses. There is never ambiguity with QUIEN/ES; it encompasses both genders, and it sounds sophisticated. It sounds sophisticated because it is the best choice. It is the best choice because grammar rules are the rules of the language (not the linguist's rules), and those rules are there to make understanding efficient and effortless.

Consider the three versions of a sentence in (14a–c) below, written by a college student in a seminar-level class on the grammatical contrasts between English and Spanish. Without thinking too much about them, choose by mere intuition the one that sounds better and the one that sounds worst. Then, read the sentences again carefully, and try to determine whether there is a difference in meaning, and what is – most probably – what the writer intended to express. If you can determine what the writer intended to express, you should be able to determine which is the sentence that should have been written. These sentences are not translated yet, so readers can do the exercise before reading the explanation.

(14) a.  *El antecedente es el sustantivo que modifica la cláusula adjetival.*[8]
     b.  *El antecedente es el sustantivo al que modifica la cláusula adjetival.*
     c.  *El antecedente es el sustantivo al cual modifica la cláusula adjetival.*

Sentence (14c) is the best one because the sentence is nonrestrictive and *el cual* is the nonrestrictive relative pronoun (see Table 2.3). Sentence (14b) might be the most frequent one, because speakers do not always obey restrictivity, particularly when it appears that there is no difference in meaning.[9] (14b) implies that there is more than one antecedent, which is clearly incorrect. Sentence (14a) is the worst because it suggests that the noun modifies the adjectival clause, the opposite of what the speaker means, as the reader will understand with help from the glosses in English in (16a–c) below. Interestingly, the *a* that appears in (14b,c) is the same "accusative *a*" that is required in Spanish when the direct object is animate and definite, as in (15b):

(15) a. *\*Alicia vio Teresa en el parque.*
'Alice saw Theresa in the park'.
b. *Alicia vio a Teresa en el parque.*
'Alice saw Theresa in the park'.

Without going into much detail, the *a* is required because Teresa is as animate (and definite) as the subject, and the latter might have been the one who saw Alicia. By a similar reasoning, the string *el sustantivo* 'the noun' is as inanimate as *la cláusula adjetival* 'the adjectival clause', and the *a* is required to distinguish the modified (*el sustantivo*) from the modifier (*la cláusula adjetival*). The "accusative *a*" is almost as required when both subject and object are inanimate and definite as when both are animate and definite. See Whitley & González (2016: 80) for an explanation of "accusative *a*" based on the animacy hierarchy in Silverstein (1976).

The equivalents in English of (14a–c) would be as follows. Readers should observe the difference in word order between (16a) and (16b).

(16) a. The antecedent is the noun that modifies [the adjectival clause[modified]].
b. The antecedent is the noun that [the adjectival clause modifies[modifier]].
c. *The antecedent is the noun to which the adjectival clause modifies.[10]

Observe that English does not have the need to codify the distinction between *that* (in 16a,b) or *which* (in 16c). Word order indicates in (16b) what the speaker wants to state (i.e. that the adjectival clause is the modifier, not the modified). In fact, a deep understanding of "accusative *a*" helps us understand why in Spanish *una cláusula adjetival modifica **a** su antecedente* but in English *an adjectival clause modifies its antecedent* (not *to* its antecedent).

Consider now (17), based on a sentence written by a student:[11]

(17) *\*La chica que le gusta George Clooney.*[12]

Sentence (17) is uninterpretable. It is impossible to determine whether the student wanted to communicate that the girl likes George Clooney or whether the student wanted to communicate that George Clooney likes the girl. Observe the difference in meaning due to the difference in relative pronoun (*a quien* vs. *que*):

(18) a. *La chica a quien le gusta George Clooney.*
    b. *La chica que le gusta a George Clooney.*[13]
    c. *George Clooney le gusta a esa chica.* (= 18a)
    d. *A esa chica le gusta George Clooney.* (= 18a)
    e. *A George Clooney le gusta esa chica.* (= 18b)
    f. *Esa chica le gusta a George Clooney.* (= 18b)

Here are the translations into English of the sentences in (18a–f):

(19) a. The girl who likes George Clooney.
    b. The girl whom George Clooney likes.
    c. That girl likes George Clooney. (= 19a)
    d. That girl likes George Clooney. (= 19a)
    e. George Clooney likes that girl. (= 19b)
    f. George Clooney likes that girl. (That girl, George Clooney likes her). (= 19b)

Let us consider now the sentences in (20a,b) and (21a,b). The reader is invited to determine which of the two sentences in each pair makes sense according to what we know about the Sun and peppers. Readers might want to time themselves and not read the next paragraph until they try to understand (20a,b). It will be clear why soon. Readers will see a translation later. Thus, start your timer and see whether you can determine which of the two sentences makes sense (both are grammatically correct).

(20) a. *Los pimientos le gustan al sol.*
    b. *El sol les gusta a los pimientos.*

In order to create some space between this pair of sentences and the following one, let us provide two beautiful quotes with adjectival clauses. The first sentence is by Mario Benedetti, a Uruguayan writer. He writes, "*me gustaría pasar el resto de mis días con alguien que no me necesite para nada, pero que me quiera para todo*". (I would like to spend the rest of my days with someone who would not need me for anything, but who would want me for everything). The second is a beautiful sentence that one of my students brought to class one day when I asked them to look up a few adjectival clauses and bring them to our discussion: "*No sé si es la mañana la que te ilumina a ti o si eres tú quien ilumina la mañana*". (I do not know whether it is the morning the one shining over you, or whether it is you who lights up the morning).

If you kept track of how much time it took for you to determine which of the two sentences in (20) is the one that makes sense (according to what we know about the Sun and peppers), try now to do the same for these two sentences. Start your timer and see whether you can determine which of the two sentences makes sense.

(21) a. *Al sol le gustan los pimientos.*
    b. *A los pimientos les gusta el sol.*

If you figured out the difference in meaning the first time, you will also see it right away in (21a,b). If you could not see the difference in (20a,b), you might have seen it in (21a,b). Consider (22a,b) before reading the answer to (20–21), and an explanation. Most readers who know some Spanish should be able to determine intuitively which of the following two sentences is more common. There is a high probability that they have read or heard sentences similar to one of them with a higher frequency. That frequency might be close to 100% for some readers, particularly for L2 learners of Spanish:

(22) a. *El chocolate me gusta.*[14]
    b. *Me gusta el chocolate.*

The fact that at least 80% of the students at the Intermediate level in the ACTFL scale (A1 to B1.2 in the CEFR scale) will answer that the frequency of (22b) is higher than that of (22a) leads to the prediction that L2 learners of Spanish will understand (21a,b) in a shorter time than (20a,b).[15] It is also possible that some readers might not be able to tell the difference between (20a,b), but some of those same readers will be able to see the difference between (21a,b). The reason is that in sentences with an indirect object and a subject, the order in (21a,b) and (22b) is much more frequent than the order in (22a) and in (20a,b). When the grammatical indirect object is animate and the subject is inanimate, Spanish tends to cast the indirect object before the verb and the subject after it (Whitley & González 2016: 111, 412). It is clear that Spanish privileges an animate indirect object (human, animal, deity) by casting it in preverbal position when the subject is inanimate. This occurs not only with an indirect object but also with a direct object (Whitley & González 2016: 412).

Finally, the reader is invited to read carefully these examples of adjectival clauses that include a preposition. These examples will help with the exercises that will follow. Most of these examples use *el que/la que*. Since in most of the cases the antecedent is a single referent, the best relative pronoun should be *el cual/la cual*. These examples will be presented again below with an alternative relative pronoun for the reader to decide which of the options is the best, according to the understanding of (non)restrictivity explained in this chapter. All of these sentences are examples given in RAE (2010), as indicated below:

(23) Acaban de hacer público un trabajo en la revista JAMA de la semana pasada en el que se establece que las llamadas bombas de insulina son más cómodas [...] (RAE 2010: 838)

(24) Me imagino que Cristo, conducido por el Demonio a la cumbre de una montaña desde la que le exhibe todas las tentaciones del mundo, sabía muy bien [...] (RAE 2010: 840)

(25) Esta es la razón por la cual toda interpretación de un acto de conducta va más allá de toda evidencia. (RAE 2010: 840)

(26) [...] Como si le diera más vergüenza la visión de la prenda íntima que la del cuerpo derribado y semidesnudo con el que la prenda había estado en contacto hasta hacía muy poco. (RAE 2010: 840)

(27) Las razones que le habían llevado a tomar una decisión tan drástica [...] no eran muy diferentes de las que me había explicado el día en que me dejó [...] (RAE 2010: 840)

(28) Se puso a coquetear con quienes la festejaban. (RAE 2010: 841)

(29) Alguna quiere que nos dé la cifra a que están reducidos los fieles. (RAE 2010: 841)

(30) El rosario de violencias con que la había castigado en los últimos meses [...] (RAE 2010: 841)

(31) —Sí –respondió con toda la sangre fría de que era capaz [...] (RAE 2010: 841)

(32) Completamente dedicado a sí mismo, no advirtió el sobresalto de Laura ni la ansiedad en que iba envuelta su siguiente pregunta. (RAE 2010: 841)

**Exercise 2.** Consider whether the second option (or the third, when available) is the best for each of the sentences. Warning: when the writer chose the best relative pronoun, the second (or third) sentence is not the best one. In the opinion of this author, the best relative pronoun was chosen in two of the ten sentences. Answers after the exercise.

1a. Acaban de hacer público un trabajo en la revista JAMA de la semana pasada **en el que** se establece que las llamadas bombas de insulina son más cómodas [...] (RAE 2010: 838)

1b. Acaban de hacer público un trabajo en la revista JAMA de la semana pasada en el cual se establece que las llamadas bombas de insulina son más cómodas [...]

2a. Me imagino que Cristo, conducido por el Demonio a la cumbre de una montaña **desde la que** le exhibe todas las tentaciones del mundo, sabía muy bien [...] (RAE 2010: 840)

2b. Me imagino que Cristo, conducido por el Demonio a la cumbre de una montaña desde la cual le exhibe todas las tentaciones del mundo, sabía muy bien [...]

3a. Esta es la razón por la cual toda interpretación de un acto de conducta va más allá de toda evidencia. (RAE 2010: 840)

3b. Esta es la razón **por la que** toda interpretación de un acto de conducta va más allá de toda evidencia.

4a. [...] Como si le diera más vergüenza la visión de la prenda íntima que la del cuerpo derribado y semidesnudo **con el que** la prenda había estado en contacto hasta hacía muy poco. (RAE 2010: 840)

4b. [...] Como si le diera más vergüenza la visión de la prenda íntima que la del cuerpo derribado y semidesnudo con el cual la prenda había estado en contacto hasta hacía muy poco.

5a. Las razones que le habían llevado a tomar una decisión tan drástica [...] no eran muy diferentes de las que me había explicado el día **en que** me dejó [...] (RAE 2010: 840)

5b. Las razones que le habían llevado a tomar una decisión tan drástica [...] no eran muy diferentes de las que me había explicado el día **en el que** me dejó [...]

5c. Las razones que le habían llevado a tomar una decisión tan drástica [...] no eran muy diferentes de las que me había explicado el día en el cual me dejó [...]

6a. Se puso a coquetear **con quienes** la festejaban. (RAE 2010: 841)

6b. Se puso a coquetear **con los que** la festejaban.

7a. Alguna quiere que nos dé la cifra **a que** están reducidos los fieles. (RAE 2010: 841)

7b. Alguna quiere que nos dé la cifra **a la que** están reducidos los fieles.

7c. Alguna quiere que nos dé la cifra a la cual están reducidos los fieles.

8a. El rosario de violencias **con que** la había castigado en los últimos meses [...] (RAE 2010: 841)

8b. El rosario de violencias **con el que** la había castigado en los últimos meses [...]

8c. El rosario de violencias con el cual la había castigado en los últimos meses [...]

9a. —Sí –respondió con toda la sangre fría **de que** era capaz ... (RAE 2010: 841)

9b. —Sí –respondió con toda la sangre fría **de la que** era capaz [...]

9c. —Sí –respondió con toda la sangre fría de la cual era capaz [...]

10a. Completamente dedicado a sí mismo, no advirtió el sobresalto de Laura ni la ansiedad **en que** iba envuelta su siguiente pregunta. (RAE 2010: 841)

10b. Completamente dedicado a sí mismo, no advirtió el sobresalto de Laura ni la ansiedad **en la que** iba envuelta su siguiente pregunta.

10c. Completamente dedicado a sí mismo, no advirtió el sobresalto de Laura ni la ansiedad <u>en la cual</u> iba envuelta su siguiente pregunta.

**Answers to exercise 2.** The best choice of relative pronoun in these sentences is always the one with *preposition* + *article* + *cual* or *preposition* + *quien/quienes* (1b, 2b, 3a, 4b, 5c, 6a, 7c, 8c, 9c, 10c). The sentences that already had the best relative pronoun are (3a) and (6a).

**Exercise 3.** Determine whether each *italicized* clause is nonrestrictive or restrictive. Most of these sentences were written by college students of Spanish as an L2. The sentences have the best relative pronoun depending on whether they are nonrestrictive or restrictive. Answers after the exercise.

1. El árbol tenía ramas *que llegaban a la ventana de mi cuarto.*
2. No hay una revisión del historial criminal del comprador, *lo cual permite que algunos criminales compren armas.*
3. Mis primos *que viven en Fort Myers* llegaron a la casa.
4. Mis primos, *quienes viven en Fort Myers,* llegaron a la casa.
5. Le guiñé el ojo a mi hermano, *quien todavía estaba en estado de "shock".*
6. Vivo en la residencia Poteat, *la cual está en una localización muy central.*
7. Me gusta la ubicación de mi habitación porque está en la esquina del edificio, *lo cual significa que tengo dos vistas distintas desde la ventana.*
8. Es lo que le digo a la gente *que me pregunta por qué quiero estudiar medicina.*
9. Descansé en mi cama y miré una película con mi papá, mientras mis amigos pasaban un buen rato en una fiesta *a la cual no pude ir.*
10. Los animales *que son mamíferos* tienen la sangre caliente.
11. En el hotel *en el cual nos alojamos* no había agua caliente.
12. Los adjetivos *que van después del sustantivo* son restrictivos.
13. La razón *por la cual la serie ha obtenido tanto éxito* es su atractivo para lectores de todas las edades.
14. La trama de la novela es solo una parte de la razón *por la cual esta obra ha tenido tanto éxito.*
15. Hay varias escenas *en las cuales los soldados matan niños de una manera brutal.*

16. Trabajan en un complot para vengarse del gobierno *por lo que ha hecho con la ayuda de Sarah Fenn.*

17. La película muestra vívida y lindamente la sombría y oscura ciudad de Gotham, *lo cual añade al tema general de la oscuridad.*

18. La película *Everest* tiene éxito cuando permite que la acción sea *la que habla,* en vez de ser los personajes quienes hablan.

19. El autor hace hincapié *en lo que se puede hacer para ayudarles a aquellos a quienes amamos.*

20. El autor hace hincapié en lo que se puede hacer por aquellos *a quienes amamos.*

21. *Lo que más me molestó* fue la forma en la cual lo dijo.

22. Lo que más me molestó fue la forma *en la cual lo dijo.*

23. El director hace hincapié en los horrores de la guerra en una escena *en la cual el francotirador debe dispararle a un niño.*

24. El director hace hincapié en los horrores de la guerra en una escena en la cual el francotirador debe dispararle a un niño *que tiene una granada en la mano.*

25. El director hace hincapié en los horrores de la guerra en una escena en la cual el francotirador debe dispararle a Rubén, *quien tiene una granada en la mano.*

26. La oración es *la que es transitiva o intransitiva*; el verbo puede usarse transitiva o intransitivamente.

27. [...] examinando otro tratamiento transformacional más completo de los adjetivos según Marta Luján, *quien ofrece la explicación más reciente y completa del fenómeno.*

28. El primer paso es deshidratar la fruta *que se va a usar,* lo cual se puede hacer de varias maneras.

29. El primer paso es deshidratar la fruta que se va a usar, *lo cual se puede hacer de varias maneras.*

30. *Lo que te voy a contar* es lo que pasó después.

**Answers to exercise 3:**

The nonrestrictive clauses are: 2, 4, 5, 6, 7, 9, 11, 13, 14, 15, 17, 22, 23, 25, 27, 29.

**Exercise 4.** The following sentences come from readings from the CVC (2020). Sentences with a relative pronoun were separated into two possible sentences that the learner will combine into one by using the best relative pronoun. For example, given these two sentences, the learner combines them into one by using the best relative pronoun. Answers after the exercise.

Example: Lisa tiene una gran pieza. Una gran pieza sirve de comedor, salón y cocina.

Answer: Lisa tiene una gran pieza que sirve de comedor, salón y cocina.

1. Forastero es la persona. La persona viene de afuera.
2. Hoguera es un fuego. Un fuego se hace en el suelo y al aire libre.
3. Un rito muy antiguo de origen pagano. Repiten un rito cada año.
4. Los metí en un saco roto. Encontré un saco roto en un rincón.
5. Tenía frente a mí un camino. Un camino llevaba al campo.
6. Los hombres salían de sus casas antes de amanecer y volvían por la tarde. Los hombres iban al campo.
7. Los esconderé en una caseta vieja. En la Alameda hay una caseta vieja.
8. Lisa mira impaciente a todos los viajeros. Todos los viajeros salen con sus maletas y sus bolsas de viaje.
9. El regalo de cumpleaños de Alicia, su mamá, es el billete para Cuba. Su mamá trabaja en una peluquería de lujo.
10. Lisa tiene una gran pieza. Una gran pieza sirve de comedor, salón y cocina.
11. Diego, el protagonista, tenía en su pieza de La Habana Vieja a todos esos santos-*orishas*. Tú estás hablando de esos santos-*orishas*.
12. Lo dice el primo Osvaldo. El primo Osvaldo es médico.
13. Hay enfermedades de los ojos. [Esas] Enfermedades de los ojos solo se curan aquí.
14. [Este libro] Explica de forma sencilla, cercana y amena el modo. Cada uno de nosotros podemos liberarnos de las cadenas que nos impiden ser libres y tomar las riendas de nuestra vida en el modo.
15. [La primera parte es] El viejo paradigma. En el viejo paradigma se hace una radiografía de la sociedad actual.
16. [La segunda parte es] El cambio de paradigma. En el cambio de paradigma se introducen claves de autoconocimiento para cuestionar el cambio de creencias con el que fuimos condicionados.
17. Se introducen claves de autoconocimiento para cuestionar el sistema de creencias. Fuimos condicionados con el sistema de creencias.
18. [La tercera parte es] El nuevo paradigma. En el nuevo paradigma se describe cómo son, piensan y actúan las personas que ya han cambiado de mentalidad.
19. En el nuevo paradigma se describe cómo son, piensan y actúan las personas. Las personas ya han cambiado de mentalidad.
20. [Este libro] Está escrito para todas aquellas personas. Todas aquellas personas están despertando.

**Answers to exercise 4:**

21. Forastero es la persona. La persona viene de afuera.
    Forastero es la persona que viene de afuera.
    (Forastero es una persona que viene de afuera.)
    (Forastero es quien viene de afuera.)
22. Hoguera es un fuego. Un fuego se hace en el suelo y al aire libre.
    Hoguera es un fuego que se hace en el suelo y al aire libre.
23. Un rito muy antiguo de origen pagano. Repiten un rito cada año.
    Un rito muy antiguo de origen pagano que repiten cada año.
    Un rito muy antiguo de origen pagano, el cual repiten cada año.
    Cada año repiten un rito muy antiguo de origen pagano. (Without an adjectival clause. In fact, this sentence is the result of omitting *que es*).
24. Los metí en un saco roto. Encontré un saco roto en un rincón.
    Los metí en un saco roto que encontré en un rincón.
    (En un rincón encontré un saco roto en el cual los metí.)
25. Tenía frente a mí un camino. Un camino llevaba al campo.
    Tenía frente a mí un camino que llevaba al campo.
26. Los hombres salían de sus casas antes de amanecer y volvían por la tarde. Los hombres iban al campo.
    Los hombres, quienes iban al campo, salían de sus casas antes del amanecer y volvían por la tarde.
27. Los esconderé en una caseta vieja. En la Alameda hay una caseta vieja.
    En la Alameda hay una caseta vieja en la cual los esconderé.
    Los esconderé en una caseta vieja que hay en la Alameda.
28. Lisa mira impaciente a todos los viajeros. Todos los viajeros salen con sus maletas y sus bolsas de viaje.
    Lisa mira impaciente a todos los viajeros, quienes salen con sus maletas y sus bolsas de viaje.
29. El regalo de cumpleaños de Alicia, su mamá, es el billete para Cuba. Su mamá trabaja en una peluquería de lujo.
    El regalo de cumpleaños de Alicia, su mamá, quien trabaja en una peluquería de lujo, es el billete para Cuba.
30. Lisa tiene una gran pieza. Una gran pieza sirve de comedor, salón y cocina.
    Lisa tiene una gran pieza, la cual sirve de comedor, salón y cocina.
    Lisa tiene una gran pieza que sirve de comedor, salón y cocina.
31. Diego, el protagonista, tenía en su pieza de La Habana Vieja a todos esos santos-*orishas*. Tú estás hablando de esos santos-*orishas*.
    Diego, el protagonista, tenía en su pieza de la Habana Vieja a todos esos santos-*orishas* de los cuales tú estás hablando.[16]

32. Lo dice el primo Osvaldo. El primo Osvaldo es médico.
    Lo dice el primo Osvaldo, quien es médico.
33. Hay enfermedades de los ojos. [Esas] Enfermedades de los ojos solo se curan aquí.
    Hay enfermedades de los ojos que solo se curan aquí.
34. [Este libro] Explica de forma sencilla, cercana y amena el modo. Cada uno de nosotros podemos liberarnos de las cadenas que nos impiden ser libres y tomar las riendas de nuestra vida en el modo.
    [Este libro] Explica de forma sencilla, cercana y amena el modo en el cual cada uno de nosotros podemos liberarnos de las cadenas que nos impiden ser libres y tomar las riendas de nuestra vida.
35. [La primera parte es] El viejo paradigma. En el viejo paradigma se hace una radiografía de la sociedad actual.
    [La primera parte es] El viejo paradigma en el cual se hace una radiografía de la sociedad actual.
36. [La segunda parte es] El cambio de paradigma. En el cambio de paradigma se introducen claves de autoconocimiento para cuestionar el sistema de creencias con el que fuimos condicionados.
    [La segunda parte es] El cambio de paradigma en el cual se introducen claves de autoconomiento para cuestionar el sistema de creencias con el que fuimos condicionados.[17]
37. Se introducen claves de autoconocimiento para cuestionar el sistema de creencias. Fuimos condicionados con el sistema de creencias.
    Se introducen claves de autoconocimiento para cuestionar el sistema de creencias con el cual fuimos condicionados.
38. [La tercera parte es] El nuevo paradigma. En el nuevo paradigma se describe cómo son, piensan y actúan las personas que ya han cambiado de mentalidad.
    [La tercera parte es] El nuevo paradigma en el cual se describe cómo son, piensan y actúan las personas que ya han cambiado de mentalidad.
39. En el nuevo paradigma se describe cómo son, piensan y actúan las personas. Las personas ya han cambiado de mentalidad.
    En el nuevo paradigma se describe cómo son, piensan y actúan quienes ya han cambiado de mentalidad. (Observe that *quienes = las personas que*.)
40. [Este libro] Está escrito para todas aquellas personas. Todas aquellas personas están despertando.
    [Este libro] Está escrito para quienes están despertando. (Observe that *quienes = todas aquellas personas que*.)

This section has shown why the generic relative pronoun *que* (the prototypical restrictive pronoun) misses the nonrestrictiveness coded when a prepositional phrase (*de Gloria*) follows an antecedent (*el hijo*), as shown with sentences (10) and (11) in §2.4. It has also shown when *article + cual/ cuales* (or *quien/quienes*, when appropriate) is preferred to *que* or *los que, las que*. It has also invited the reader to do exercises based on sentences produced by L2 learners of Spanish, sentences from RAE (2010), and sentences from readings from the Centro Virtual Cervantes. Readers saw and practiced with dozens of adjectival clauses in which a prepositional phrase follows the antecedent. These adjectival clauses are particularly challenging for L2 learners whose first language is English because of the need to avoid *preposition stranding* (*about* in *what are you talking about* is stranded), a tough assignment when practice with adjectival clauses with prepositional phrases is limited to a couple of isolated examples or to two or three sentences in an exercise with ten items.

After the practice and all of the examples in this chapter and in Chapter 1, no reader should have any doubt now why if the person visiting this week is their *guapo novio* (their only boyfriend, who is a handsome person), they are living a life without unnecessary complications. However, if the visitor is their *novio guapo* (one of their boyfriends, the one who is handsome), they are living a life that might be a little more complicated than needed.

## 2.6. Some implications for teaching

The distinction discussed in this chapter used to seem overwhelming, perhaps unteachable. Part of the problem is the issue of avoiding grammar in pedagogical materials because it seems useless or too complicated for the time allowed. Adjectival clauses is one of those points of grammar that seems elusive; perhaps less important. Or at least not the highest priority in a class where students are rushed from activity to activity, often without providing them with the necessary foundation in vocabulary and grammar to complete those class activities. If we start bringing this distinction to the attention of teachers, future generations of students will begin to get better explanations early on in their schooling. Awareness and scaffolding will go a long way.

Knowledge begins with awareness of the challenge. A teacher aware of the importance of adjectival clauses will make an effort to understand them better and teach them better. (Non)restrictiveness can be approached by scaffolding. A first step is to make the connection between simple definitions and restrictive adjectival clauses early on in schooling: a dictionary is a book *that is* used to look up the meaning of the words that one does not know. (*That + is* is left on purpose in the preceding sentence to show the full restrictive adjectival clause.) There are two restrictive clauses in the preceding definition, and all of the words in the definition can be used in an elementary textbook. If we are aware and make our students aware of this structure, we will naturally run into nonrestrictive adjectival clauses, and we will begin teaching them simply by noticing them and observing the important difference in meaning that they express.

Frantzen (2013) echoed other scholars and added her voice to the proposal to use literary examples in the teaching of grammar. Examples similar to those in Table 2.3 in this chapter began as the result of observing adjectival clauses in a reading for a class of intermediate Spanish in college. Calling attention to the meaning expressed with a restrictive adjectival clause as opposed to a nonrestrictive one can be part of the follow-up exercises for a reading. What is the difference in meaning if we change punctuation and the relative pronoun? A similar strategy can be used when teaching *ser/estar* or preterite/imperfect, as the following two chapters will show as well.

Let us finish with a brief discussion on how adjectival clauses can help L2 learners solve problems they encounter in their process of writing. One student in college wrote one of the following two sentences:

(45) a.   *Un grupo racista de hombres*
     b.   *Un grupo de hombres racistas*

Adjectival clauses immediately came to mind as a possible way to determine whether *racista* 'racist' modifies *grupo* 'group' or whether it modifies *hombres* 'men':

(46) a.   *Un grupo racista que es de hombres*
          'A racist group who is (composed) of men'
     b.   *Un grupo de hombres que son racistas*
          'A group of men who are racists'

The level of awareness that many L2 learners will develop upon the understanding of (non)restrictivity outlined in this chapter might lead many of them to *infer* that the phrase in (46b) – or the corresponding one in another language – is the correct one. There are at least two reasons. The reader will remember from §1.10 that Spanish allows the omission of *que* + *ser*. That explanation would work for both phrases. But it is clear that the restrictive relative clause *hombres que son racistas* makes good sense whereas the restrictive clause *racista que es de hombres* does not seem to add up. The second reason is that the modifier *de hombres* seems intuitively a more natural modifier for *grupo* (*grupo de hombres*) than *racista* is for *grupo* (*grupo racista*) This intuition was confirmed by Ngram Viewer (2020). The string *grupo de hombres* = 0.0000000525% in the year 2000, but the string *grupo racista* was not found.

## 2.7. Conclusions

An adjectival clause is nonrestrictive if the property that it expresses applies to all of the referents of the noun (the antecedent) that the clause modifies. The adjectival clause can be left out without affecting the meaning of the main sentence, and both sentences can stand by themselves: *my boyfriend is visiting me this week. My boyfriend is a handsome person* (*my boyfriend, who is a handsome person, is visiting me this week*). An adjectival clause is restrictive if the property that it expresses applies only to part of the referents of the noun (the antecedent) that the clause modifies. A restrictive adjectival clause cannot be left out without affecting the meaning of the main sentence, and the adjectival clause does not stand on its own. The strings *a hammer is a tool* and *a tool is used to drive nails* can be combined into *a hammer is a tool (that is) used to drive nails*. No speaker of English utters the string *a tool is used to drive nails* in isolation because it would imply that the main use of any tool is driving nails. However, the adjectival clause *that is used to drive nails* as a modifier of *a tool* restricts or limits the use of a tool called *hammer* to a type of tool used primarily to drive nails. That restrictive adjectival clause distinguishes a hammer from any other possible tool.

This chapter also showed that the main difference between sentences similar to *el hijo de Gloria, <u>el cual es ingeniero ecológico</u>, trabaja en el gobierno* y *el hijo de Gloria, **el que es ingeniero ecológico**, trabaja en el gobierno* is that the first sentence refers to the totality of Gloria's sons (by entailing that Gloria has just one son), whereas the second one refers to a part of Gloria's sons (by entailing that Gloria has at least two sons). That is, the first sentence is nonrestrictive and the second one is restrictive. Remember that a sentence A entails a sentence B if every time that A is true, B is true. Thus, the listener or reader can draw an inference if the speaker or writer properly coded totality or part by using the relative pronoun that expresses the intended meaning. How does one know whether Gloria has one or two sons or other children? No listener/reader needs to know this. However, any listener/reader can draw the correct inference if the speaker/writer used the relative pronoun that allows readers to do precisely that. That is how a good speaker or writer communicates more than meets the eye. Or the ear, for that matter. That is the reason why the generic relative pronoun *que* might suffice, but it might not always be the most informative choice; that is, the choice that allows the listener/reader to distinguish between whole and part when the distinction matters.

To put together Chapter 1 and Chapter 2, an adjective preceding its noun expresses totality as does a nonrestrictive adjectival clause; an adjective following its noun expresses part as does a restrictive adjectival clause. The same dichotomy is at play, and rightly so: if an adjectival clause functions like an adjective in a sentence, and the latter can be used nonrestrictively or restrictively, then the former will also be nonrestrictive or restrictive. Meaning matters.

## Notes

 1 An attentive teacher might indicate to a student that strings similar to *that is* in (1f) above can be left out of their composition (without losing any information), even if that teacher has never read that there is a rule of copula deletion (or omission of *be* in a sentence).
 2 As explained in Chapter 1, many speakers of Spanish (including native speakers) are not explicitly aware of the difference in meaning coded by the position of the adjective. Chapter 1 explains the difference, and why a more explicit understanding is lacking but very desirable.
 3 Ngrams for *the one who is beautiful* = 0.0000000277%. Oct. 30, 2019. Ngrams for *the one that is beautiful* = 0
 4 Nonrestrictive adjectival clauses (like 6a) were called in Spanish explicative by Bello (1941[1847]). That term appears to come from Latin. Robert Ulery (p.c. circa 2008) explained at a talk on adjective position that a prenominal adjective in Latin "unfolded" or "explained" the meaning of its noun.
 5 The notation [+human] means that the referent is animate; [-human], inanimate.
 6 Remember that an asterisk (*) before a string of words means that it is ungrammatical or that natives do not produce it.
 7 Interestingly, these four prepositions are among the five most frequent prepositions in Spanish, according to Ngram: *de* (5.8960%), *en* (2.1575%), *a* (1.5430%), *por* (0.7409%), *con* (0.6656%). (Search done in 2020.)
 8 The examples in this section were written by students (with the exception of 15, 20, 21, and 22). Example 14 came from an undergraduate seminar on Spanish/ English contrastive grammar.
 9 Ngram for *el que modifica* = 0.0000020729%
    Ngram for *el cual modifica* = 0.0000003036% (12.77% of 23765). (Search done in April 2020.)
10 An asterisk (*) before a sentence means that it is ungrammatical or not produced by native speakers.
11 What the student wrote was *mi papá le gusta mis amigas*, a sentence *which* is uninterpretable in Spanish because the reader cannot determine whether *he likes them* or *they like him*. This author changed it to the George Clooney example because many people would agree that someone is special if George Clooney likes them, but none of us is special for liking George Clooney.
12 Criado de Val (1958: 82–85), quoted by Ozete (1981: 86), discusses the encroachment of *que* instead of *quien* in sentences like *era un hombre que le gustaba divertirse*. (It should read *era un hombre a quien/al cual le gustaba divertirse*). See also Brucart (2016: 729); DeMello (1993); RAE (2010: 852); Whitley (2002: 278); among others.
13 Sentences (18a) and (18b) are not synonymous. The situation portrayed by one of those sentences is unremarkable, if one agrees that any person can like George Clooney. The situation portrayed in the other sentence is special if one agrees that being liked by George Clooney is something that many people would treasure.

14 Ngrams for *me gusta cantar* = 0.0000008646% in 2000.
  Ngrams for *cantar me gusta* = 0. (Search done in December 2019.)
15 This author has asked that question to students during the last three years at least, and most of them answered right away that (22b) is what speakers of Spanish would say.
16 This sentence seems to be an interesting case of a nonrestrictive adjectival clause not preceded by a comma. It might be that *preposition + article + cuales* makes punctuation unnecessary. This is an issue for further research.
17 This author would write *el sistema de creencias con el cual fuimos condicionados*.

## References

Bello, Andrés. 1941 [1847]. *Gramática de la lengua castellana*. With notes by Rufino J. Cuervo. Buenos Aires: Librería Perlado Editores.

Brucart, José María. 2016. Oraciones de relativo. In Gutiérrez-Rexach, Javier (ed.), *Enciclopedia de lingüística hispánica*, vol 2, 722–736. London: Routledge. (https://www.routledge.com/9781138941380)

Butt, John & Benjamin, Carmen. 1988. *A new reference grammar of modern Spanish*. London: Edward Arnold.

CVC (Centro Virtual Cervantes). 2020. (https://cvc.cervantes.es) (Last accessed 2020)

DeMello, George. 1993. Pronombre relativo con antecedente humano. *Nueva Revista de Filología Hispánica* 41. 75–98. (http://www.jstor.com/stable/40299210)

Dozier, Eleanor & Iguina, Zulma. 2017. Manual de gramática. *Grammar reference for students of Spanish*, 6th ed. Boston: Cengage Learning. (Instructor's edition).

Frantzen, Diana. 2013. Using literary texts to reveal problematic rules of usage. *Foreign Language Annals* 46. 628–645. (https://doi.org/10.1111/flan.12057)

Gili Gaya, Samuel. 1985[1961]. *Curso superior de sintaxis española*. 15th reprint. Barcelona: Biblograf.

Lunn, Patricia Vinning & DeCesaris, Janet A. 2007. *Investigación de gramática*, 2nd ed. Boston: Thomson Heinle.

Ngram Viewer. 2020. (https://books.google.com/ngrams)

Ozete, Óscar. 1981. Current usage of adjectival pronouns in Spanish. *Hispania* 64. 85–91. (https://www.jstor.org/stable/34033)

RAE (Real Academia Española y Asociación de Academias de la Lengua Española). 2010. *Nueva gramática de la lengua española. Manual*. Madrid: Espasa. Printed by Editorial Planeta Colombiana SA, Bogotá. (https://www.rae.es/obras-acade micas/gramatica/manual-de-la-nueva-gramatica)

Silverstein, Michael. 1976. Hierarchy of features and ergativity. In Dixon, R.M. (ed.), *Grammatical categories in Australian languages*, 112–171. Canberra: Australian Institute of Aboriginal Studies.

Whitley, M. Stanley. 2002. *Spanish/English contrasts. A course in Spanish linguistics*, 2nd ed. Washington: Georgetown University Press.

Whitley, M. Stanley & González, Luis. 2016. *Gramática para la composición*, 3rd. ed. Washington: Georgetown University Press. (http://press.georgetown.edu/bo ok/languages/gramática-para-la-composición-0)

# 3 *Estar* expresses change of state; most learners already have *ser* in their native language

*Luis H. González and Michael Davern*

## 3.1. Introduction

Bull (1965: 292) writes, "In other words, *estar* implies a change to whatever is described by the predicate adjective". It is clear that scholars have not read Bull's rule for predicate adjectives with the attention that it deserves because its powerful predictions have not been applied in textbooks for Spanish as a second language (L2). Bull's twelve-word statement can be expressed in six words: *ESTAR expresses a change of state*. Furthermore, this statement is a lot more encompassing than Bull might have thought because not only does it account for *estar* + adjective; it accounts for three other rules invoked for *estar* in a typical textbook: change in location, sentences in the progressive aspect, and resultative sentences. As Whitley & González (2016: 32) observe, change of state also accounts for a number of what some textbooks call "idiomatic expressions" with *estar* (Lequerica de la Vega & Salazar 2006: 101–102; Dozier & Iguina 2017: 274; among others), a point addressed in §3.5 below. Each of the sentences in (1a–i) exemplifies the result of a change or the IMPLICATURE that a change is expected to happen (1j,k):[1]

(1) a. *El gato Tutti Frutti está asustado/bien/castrado/dormido/emocio-nado/flaco/gordo.*
'The cat Tutti Frutti is frightened/well/castrated/asleep/excited/thin/fat'. (With the intent that the cat appears (or is) frightened/well/castrated/asleep/excited/thin/fat.)

b. *Tutti Frutti estuvo enfermo un par de semanas.*
'Tutti Frutti was sick for two weeks'.

c. *Ahora está muerto.*
'Now he is dead'.

d. *Está enterrado debajo de un helecho.*
'He is buried under a fern'.

e. *La camisa está planchada/sucia/lavada/arrugada.*
   'The shirt is ironed/dirty/washed/wrinkled'.
f. *Hoy, la Ciudad de Chicago está paralizada por la nieve.*
   'Today, the City of Chicago is paralyzed by snow'.
g. *Estoy impresionada.*
   'I am impressed'.
h. *La pintura está detrás de la puerta.*
   'The paint is behind the door'.
i. *La pintora está pintando la puerta.*
   'The painter is painting the door'.
j. *Esa puerta estaba sin pintar ayer.*
   'That door was without paint(ing) yesterday'.
k. *La puerta estará pintada en una hora.*
   'The door will be painted in an hour'.

In the examples above, each use of *estar* expresses a change. Since the notion of *state* is central in language (states is one of the main four types of verbs, as per Vendler 1957), this chapter will refer to *change of state* from now on.

This chapter will systematically apply the use of *estar* as change of state to several rules common in textbooks in order to show that Bull's simplified rule is more encompassing than he thought. This chapter is organized as follows. It will begin with change of location (§3.2), move to the passive voice and resultant states (§3.3), then to the progressive (§3.4), and finally to "idiomatic expressions" (§3.5). Following these explanations, it will briefly address the proposal in VanPatten (2010: 35) that teaching should privilege *estar* because *ser* "will largely take care of itself" (§3.6). It will finish with some implications for the teaching of Spanish as an L2 (§3.7), followed by conclusions (§3.8).

Whitley (2002: 315) observed that Bull was the first scholar to see the difference in "predicate adjectives" as a contrast between the norm and a change. Bull had proposed that explanation in Bull (1942: 435), and he gives credit to Alonso & Henríquez Ureña (1941: 123–124) when they wrote, "El adjetivo […] con *estar* significa […] que la cualidad se da como un estado alcanzado. *Estar* quiere decir 'ponerse, volverse delgado, o colérico, o blanco, o frío […]'"

Let us explain the norm and change of state with this example. Cousin Carlos had always known Uncle Fernando as an obese person. As far as he knows, Uncle Fernando is obese (*él es gordo*). However, Uncle Fernando had a heart attack, his doctor put him on a strict diet, he is following it, and he has lost 80 pounds since Carlos last saw him. Upon seeing him now, Carlos can say *el tío Fernando está muy flaco* 'Uncle Fernando is very skinny'. On the other hand, Cousin Lina, who never knew Uncle Fernando when he was obese, can say *el tío Fernando es muy flaco* 'Uncle Fernando is very skinny'. Cousin Carlos expressed a change with *estar* when Uncle Fernando went from 220 pounds to 140 pounds. Lina has not seen a change, and she is not expressing a change; she is expressing the norm for Uncle Fernando, as far as she knows. Both cousins are correct. The difference is that Carlos has some knowledge of the world that Lina does not have. He is expressing *what he knows* and what he sees; she can express only what she sees. He is expressing a change of state; she is expressing the norm. The rest of this chapter will show that a rule of *estar* as expressing a change of state is the rule at work not only with (predicate) adjectives; it also accounts for three other uses of *estar*.

## 3.2.  A change in location is a change of state

If someone went outside, he or she changed location. Since a change in location is uncontroversially a change of state, the observation that *estar* expresses a change of state leads to the prediction that stating that someone is now outside must be expressed with *estar*. That prediction is correct.

(2)   *El gato está afuera.*
      'The cat is outside'. (cf. *\*el gato es afuera*).[2]

Indeed, expressing location is the first rule for *estar* introduced in two textbooks for elementary Spanish consulted right after we wrote this example (*Sol y viento* and *¡Anda!*). Since a change of location is a change of state, this explanation accounts for a putative rule of change of location with a rule that the grammar of Spanish already has for sentences (1a–g), and countless similar sentences.

An attendee at a conference where this proposal was presented in February 2019 asked how can this explanation account for the observation that someone might say that their *gatitas Mila y Nica están adentro* 'their kittens Mila and Nica are inside', when those kittens have never been outside. In that sense, to be inside is the norm (not a change) for those kittens, but no native speaker says *las gatitas son adentro* 'the kittens are inside'. First, *adentro* 'inside' and *afuera* 'outside' are adverbs of place in Spanish. By virtue of being adverbs of place, they express location. Second, *adentro* and *afuera* are inseparable, as the two sides of a coin, to borrow the image for a linguistic sign from the famous French linguist Ferdinand de Saussure, as if a speaker cannot use one without conjuring up the other. Third, it is uncontroversial that expressing that a referent is outside or inside when those two words are used in their primary adverbial function is expressing a change of location, and therefore the prediction is that such a change will require *estar*. In fact, *adentro* 'inside' and *afuera* 'outside' are more often than not used to express a change in location. The Ngrams for *es adentro* 'is inside' was 0.0000017869%, the Ngrams for *está adentro* 'is inside' was 0.0000165382%; that is, the latter is almost ten times more frequent than the former (Ngram Viewer 2020). Similar data were obtained for *es afuera* 'is outside' = 0.0000022558% and for *está afuera* 'is outside' = 0.0000233027%. It is possible to say that someone's kittens *SON gaticas domésticas que nunca han ESTADO afuera* 'are inside kittens that have never been outside'. (cf. *Nunca han sido afuera). The following section explains why it is also possible to say that *la boda será afuera* 'la boda will be (celebrated) outside', although the priest or judge officiating it *estará afuera* 'will be outside' and s/he will never *será afuera* 'will be outside'.

### 3.3. Why an explicit understanding of passive voice (and resultant state) is an efficient use of classroom time

Consider these two sentences:

(3) a. *La puerta fue cerrada.* → past voice
    'The door was closed'. (By someone/something.)
  b. *La puerta estaba cerrada.*
    'The door was closed'.

If a teacher asks in a college class of Spanish as an L2 (e.g. first semester to third semester) whether the two sentences above show a difference in meaning, some students might know that there is a difference, and some of them might know what it is. Some students might not be able to see any difference. After all, the corresponding sentence in English appears to be the same. Now, the teacher can use the following sentences:

(4) a. *La puerta fue abierta.*
    'The door was opened'. (By someone/something.)
  b. *La puerta estaba abierta.*
    'The door was open'.

This time, some of the students who did not know the difference in meaning in (3a,b) will begin to understand it (due to the difference between *opened* and *open*). If asked to explain the difference, some students might say that one of the sentences expresses an action, or that someone did something. Or, better yet, that something was done. No need to speculate as to what students will say about the other sentence. Most readers will know that one of the sentences is the passive voice, and that said sentence is the one that expresses that something was done: the door was closed (underwent closing) or the door was opened (underwent opening). That is the sentence with *fue*. The other sentence is called a resultative sentence; that is, a sentence expressing a resultant state. That is the sentence with *estaba*, and sentences with *estar* + past participle will invariably express a new state that resulted from an action. The passive voice and the resultant state can be paraphrased as in (5a,b) below:

(5)  a.   The door was opened. = The door underwent opening.
     b.   The door was open. = The door was in a state of opening. (The door was not closed.)

Now the reader is ready to see why the sentences on the left in Table 3.1 favor the preterite aspect of the past tense, are grammatical as written, and each would be incomplete if the present tense is used. Those sentences can be expressed in the present, but something must be added to show unequivocally that they are sentences in the passive voice. An example of what could be added to make them felicitous (grammatical and appropriate) is shown in the sentences (6a–e) below the table. On the other hand, the sentences on the right favor the present, and are grammatical as they are.[1]

*Table 3.1* Passive voice vs. resultant state

| **Passive voice**: favors the preterite. If the present tense is used, something must be added to make the sentence felicitous. | **Resultant state**: favors the present. It is complete as it is (in present tense). |
|---|---|
| *La comida fue preparada.* 'The food was prepared'. (cf. %La comida es preparada.)[3] | *La comida está preparada.* 'The food is prepared'. (The food is ready). |
| *La comida fue servida.* 'The food was served'. (cf. %La comida es servida.) | *La comida está servida.* 'The food is served'. (It is on the table.) |
| *La casa fue quemada.* 'The house was (got) burned'. (cf. %La casa es quemada.) | *La casa está quemada.* 'The house is burned'. (It is charred.) |
| *La casa fue remodelada.* 'The house was renovated'. (cf. %La casa es remodelada.) | *La casa está remodelada.* 'The house is renovated'. (It was renovated, updated.) |
| *La puerta fue abierta.* 'The door was (got) opened'. (cf. %La puerta es abierta.) | *La puerta está abierta.* 'The door is open'. |
| *Las ventanas fueron pintadas.* 'The windows were painted'. (cf. %Las ventanas son pintadas.) | *Las ventanas están pintadas.* 'The windows are painted'. (They have a coat of paint.) |

The sentences with *ser* in the present tense are incomplete, but they become grammatical if an adverbial/quantifier phrase similar to those in (6a–d) below is added (*el día antes* 'the day before', *cuando todos han llegado* 'when everyone has arrived', *cada veinte años* 'every twenty years', etc.). However, it must be pointed out that the same meaning is more often than not better expressed using the best equivalent in Spanish of the passive voice: an intransitivization with *se* (Whitley & González 2016: 88). They can also be expressed better using ANTEPOSITION (or LEFT DISLOCATION), a syntactic alternation (a syntactic option) that expresses the object (direct in this case) before the verb, as the last paraphrase in each of the sentences below shows.

(6) a. *La comida es preparada el día antes. (La comida se prepara el día antes; la comida la preparan el día antes).*
   'Dinner is prepared the day before'.
   b. *La comida es servida cuando todos han llegado. (La comida se sirve cuando todos han llegado; la comida la sirven cuando todos han llegado).*
   'Dinner is served when everybody has arrived'.
   c. *La casa es quemada (y reconstruida) para que los bomberos practiquen. (La casa se quema (y se reconstruye) para que los bomberos practiquen. La casa la queman [...]).*
   'The house is burned (and reconstructed) so firefighters can practice'.
   d. *La casa es remodelada cada 20 años. (La casa se remodela cada 20 años. La casa la remodelan cada 20 años).*
   'The house is remodeled every twenty years'.
   e. *La puerta es abierta a las 6:00 AM. (La puerta se abre a las 6:00 AM. La puerta la abren a las 6:00 AM).*
   'The door is opened at 6:00 AM'.

What Table 3.1 shows can be termed the specialization of the two copulas in Spanish: *ser + past participle* expresses the passive voice; *estar + past participle* expresses a resultant state. Indeed, a deep understanding of resultative sentences (sentences expressing a resultant state) is what led these authors to the realization that change of state is the main meaning expressed with *estar*. We had read Bull (1965) several years ago, but it takes years of teaching, dozens of questions from students, and a good understanding of the Aktionsart classes of verbs (Vendler 1957) to connect the dots as done in this chapter. Of course, an explanation of Vendler's classes of verbs (or classes of predicates) does not belong in an L2 classroom. However, passive voice – one of the most basic rules in languages, in spite of the push back in schools – is a concept that definitely belongs in the classroom, if only to warn L2 learners that Spanish often prefers an intransitivization with *se* or anteposition of the object (left dislocation), as those familiar with Spanish will recognize upon reading the two alternations in parentheses of the passive voice sentences in (6a–e) above. A better understanding of resultative sentences (resultant states) will go a long way in understanding change of state, the key notion in the understanding of *estar*. Resultative sentences and passive voice deserve attention in the classroom, and Table 3.1 is a suggestion for how to explain the differences between the two structures, even in elementary Spanish. The only words not easily inferred by anglo speakers are *abrir* 'open', *comida* 'dinner', *casa* 'house', *puerta* 'door', *quemar* 'burn', *ventana* 'window'. The only word not found among the 1,640 most frequent words in Spanish was *quemar* 'burn' (http://corpus.rae.es/frec/5000_formas.TXT).

It is uncontroversial that *estar* + participle expresses a result; therefore it expresses that a change has occurred. This is the second additional rule covered with Bull's observation that *estar* + adjective expresses a change.

*[handwritten: Estar: a change has ocurred.]*

### 3.4. If the progressive is always with *estar*, and if *estar* expresses change, then the progressive expresses an explicit (or implied) change

So far, a rule that *estar* + adjective expresses a change of state has also accounted for two common rules for *estar*: location, and resultant state. Two additional rules have been accounted for with a rule that is already part of the grammar of Spanish. VanPatten (1987, 2010) has observed that the use of *estar* to form the progressive aspect is in some studies the first rule of *estar* that L2 learners of Spanish acquire. If the rule that *estar* expresses a change of state is on the right track, and if the progressive requires *estar*, the prediction is that the progressive should signal a change of state. That prediction is correct. If readers do not see the implied change in (7a–c) – those people are doing something that is different from what they were doing a few minutes ago, and they will probably be doing something different in minutes – they sure would agree that (7d) expresses a change of state, if they have experienced that state of affairs.

(7)  a.  *La mami está tomando una siesta.*
         'Mom is taking a nap'.
     b.  *El papi está bañándose.*
         'Dad is taking a shower'.
     c.  *Los niños están jugando fútbol.*
         'The children are playing soccer'.
     d.  *El aire acondicionado no está enfriando.*
         'The air conditioning is not cooling'.

True, the progressive is always with *estar*, and that might be the better understood and more accurate use of *estar* by beginning L2 learners of Spanish. However, associating the progressive with a change of state should help L2 learners understand the more general rule of *estar* as the copula expressing change. That way, there is one fewer rule, which in turn strengthens an encompassing principle of change of state as the main meaning of *estar*. Interestingly, the progressive can be formed with other verbs in Spanish (and in other languages): *seguir* 'follow', *continuar* 'continue', *ir* 'go', *andar* 'go around', *venir* 'come', *quedar(se)* 'remain', 'stay', etc. Remarkably, when these verbs are used, no change is highlighted. Therefore, if a rule of change of state accounts for three rules invoked for *estar*, and if the progressive is always with *estar*, then the prediction is that the progressive expresses change.

The rule that *estar* + adjective expresses a change of state has covered three additional rules (change of location, resultant state, the progressive aspect), and has shown that Bull's rule is more predictive than he thought. In fact, neither Bull nor scholars during the last 55 years appear to have noticed the predictions just shown. One rule has covered what textbooks account for with four different rules.

This is a good moment to make a connection with Chapter 4, which shows that the imperfect expresses that the subject of the sentence is in the middle of an interval. Speaking somewhat loosely, one can say that the imperfect is an interval. González (2020: 33–38) provides ample evidence that approximately 20% of the uses of *por* also express an interval, not only in time (*algunos escritores prefieren escribir por la noche* 'some writers prefer to write at night'), but more frequently in space (*por el parque* 'by the park', *por el lado izquierdo* 'on the left side', etc.). Observe also that the progressive expresses an interval, as all of the sentences in (7a–d) show. That interval is ordinarily shorter in Spanish than in English. If the progressive expresses a short interval, not only are speakers expressing all of the time that folks are in the middle of intervals, but also that they are constantly entering and leaving them. Therefore, a change of state is frequently happening. To tie together this section and this paragraph, the progressive, the imperfect, and *por* all express intervals. Let us proceed with what some textbooks call idiomatic expressions with *estar*.

## 3.5. Change of state also accounts for putative "idioms" with *estar*

Lequerica de la Vega & Salazar (2006: 101–102) list 20 "frases idiomáticas" with *estar*. Dozier & Iguina (2017: 41) list 14. Whitley & González

(2016: 32) provide the following subset from those and similar lists, and they observe that every one of these phrases expresses a change.

(8)  a.  *Estar sin empleo*                    'be without work'
     b.  *Estar en huelga*                      'be on strike'
     c.  *Estar de guardia*                     'be on call/duty'
     d.  *Estar de moda*                        'be in fashion, be in'
     e.  *Estar de luto*                        'be in mourning'
     f.  *Estar de acuerdo*                     'agree, be in agreement'
     g.  *Estar de prisa*                       'be in a hurry'
     h.  *Estar de pie*                         'be standing'
     i.  *Estar de viaje/de vacaciones*         'be traveling/on vacation'
     j.  *Estar de buen humor/de mal humor* 'be in a good mood/bad mood'

Observe that none of these expressions accepts *ser*. That is a clue that they have something in common, and that they do not share this property with *ser*. Furthermore, they all express a change of state. If you are sitting down, you are in a state that has changed from your state seconds or minutes before, and you will likely have a change of state within the next few seconds or minutes; if you are kneeling down, you are in a different state; and so are you if you are standing up. In fact, *estar* comes from *stare*, the verb in Latin for 'stand'. Those three different positions (sitting, kneeling, and standing) are good examples of simple and highly frequent changes of state. If you are in a bad mood, a change has happened; if you are back (because *estaba de vacaciones* 'you were on vacation', a change of location (and daily routine/life) has happened. Therefore, if all of these expressions show a change of state, these expressions are part of a discernible pattern. If there is a pattern, they are not isolated cases; they are rule-governed. It turns out that the simplified version of Bull's rule (*estar* expresses change of state) is at work in all of these expressions, and in countless similar ones. L2 learners of Spanish do not have to memorize them if they can tell whether a change of state happened. This is what native speakers appear to be doing: "computing" change of state in the four rules reviewed and in phrases like these and in countless others.

## 3.6. Giving some teeth to the proposal in VanPatten (2010) about privileging *estar*

Attentive readers – and particularly those familiar with the issues discussed in this chapter – might be wondering why little has been said about *ser*. Bull (1942; 1965) was the first scholar to observe that *ser* + adjective expresses the norm (Whitley 2002: 315). VanPatten (1987; 2010: 33) observes that, "*ser* is three to four times more frequent in the input to learners compared with *estar*". In fact, a search of the 1,000 most frequent forms in CREA (http://corpus.rae.es/lfrecuencias.html) showed that the normalized frequency for *es* is 6,683 per million words; that of *está* is 1,565. That shows that the frequency for *es* is 4.27 times that of *está*. If the frequency in input to learners reflects the frequency in real life, *ser* is at least four times more frequent than *estar*.

A single rule that *estar* expresses change of state can now give teeth to the proposal in VanPatten (2010: 35) that the problem of teaching *ser* and *estar* is *estar* because *ser* "will largely take care of itself", conceivably for the two reasons stated in the previous paragraph: it is the norm (does not express a change of state), and it is also at least four times more frequent than *estar*. VanPatten proposes that perhaps the task of L2 teachers is to privilege *estar*. That can be done by helping L2 learners understand how *estar* expresses a change. When no change is expressed, learners should use *ser*. Interestingly, change is often the expression of a deviation from the norm. Indeed, the notion of change of state is so strong that it is *implied* in changes that have not occurred, as the reader can now understand better by going back to the examples in (1j,k), (7a–d) with progressive sentences, the phrases in (8a–j), and as the following brief discussion shows.

Suppose that a buyer goes to a supermarket where she sees two apples that are green in color. One of them is a red delicious and the other is a Granny Smith. The "visible" color of both is green. The red delicious *no es verde pero está verde* 'is not green but is unripe'; the Granny Smith *es verde pero no está verde* 'is green but is not unripe'; it might be perfectly ripe, but it will always be green in color. The following table explains that scenario in more detail.

### 3.7. Change of state explains apparently challenging (or nuanced) uses

Change of state explains why speakers of Spanish say *el abuelo está muerto* 'Grandpa is dead' and not \**el abuelo es muerto*. Dead is as permanent as it gets, but it is a change. Change of state also explains why either *ser* or *estar* is used with young/old and with single/married. As Bull (1965: 295) observed, "There are few states more temporary than being young and none more permanent than being old, yet the Spaniard describes both with either *ser* or *estar*". When *estar* is used, a changed is expressed (or at least implied); otherwise, *ser* is used. The force of change of state also explains the (relatively free) variation with *soltero* 'single' and *casado* 'married'. Interestingly, *un solterón* 'a bachelor' or *una solterona* 'a bachelorette' *es un solterón* or *es una solterona*, and never *\*estará un solterón* or *\*estará una solterona*. RAE (2018) defines *solterón/solterona* in its online dictionary as, *"una persona entrada en años y que no se ha casado"* 'a person of an advanced age and who has not married'.

(9)  a.  *Margarita está casada.*
'Margarita is married'.
(Search on Corpes XXI (*está casada*) in May 2019: 0.89 cases per million)
(Search on Corpes XXI (*está casado*) in May 2019: 1.45 cases per million)

b.  *Margarita es casada.*
'Margarita is married'.
(Search on Corpes XXI (*es casada*) in May 2019: 0.11 cases per million)
(Search on Corpes XXI (*es casado*) in May 2019: 0.28 cases per million)

c.  *El tío Jorge, quien tiene 48 años, es un solterón.*
'Uncle Jorge, who is 48, is a bachelor'.

d.  *\*El tío Jorge, quien tiene 48 años, está un solterón.*
(Search on Corpes XXI (*está un solterón*) in May 2019: 0 cases)
(Search on Corpes XXI (*es un solterón*) in May 2019: 4 cases)

Although being married while in graduate school might not be the norm, it is common for a few graduate students to be married. However, if one finds out that a 20-year old undergraduate student is already married, one can expect the following question, asked with some surprise:

(10)  *¿Esa estudiante (tan joven) ya está casada?*
'Is that student (who looks so young) already married?'

The surprise comes from a change that is a deviation from the norm. Neither of the authors, one of them a native speaker, sees himself using *es casada* in the previous question.

To summarize this section, *es/está casada/o* are both used by native speakers because being married can refer to a change of state or to the norm, depending on context. This is another case of the force of the intuition of change of state, including impending change, as the examples with the progressive, the ones with the apples, and sentences (1j,k) and (7a–d) show.

A rule that *estar* expresses a change of state also accounts for the explanation in Falk (1979: 74) of *ser* + adjective vs. *estar* + adjective as a comparison of a referent with other members of her class (*Lina es bonita* 'Lina is pretty'), as opposed to comparing that referent with herself (*hoy Lina está más bonita que nunca* 'Today, Lina is (looks) prettier than ever'). Franco & Steinmetz (1983) discuss a proposal, basically identical, but without giving credit to Falk. Conceivably, they arrived independently at the same analysis. Carlson (1977) had proposed the now widely invoked distinction between individual-level predicates (expressed with *ser*) and stage-level predicates (expressed with *estar*). It appears that scholars working on Hispanic linguistics were not aware of it until years later, since Silva-Corvalán (1986) does not quote Carlson, either. Since the notion of change of state is something that can be used in the classroom because it is understood by undergraduate students (this explanation has been tested with undergraduate students for the past fifteen years), these authors decided to leave out a theoretical discussion of individual-level/stage-level predicates (Carlson 1977). The questions of whether Carlson's distinction is needed in the classroom, whether it can be used, and whether it contributes anything that is not already covered by change of state are left for future research. Consider, for example, the contrast discussed in Pastor (2016: 374) between *mi coche es rojo* 'my car is red' (individual-level predicate) and *las hojas del roble están rojas* 'the oak's leaves are red' (stage-level predicate [with the intended meaning 'have turned red' or 'are now red']). The first sentence does not express a change, and it takes *ser*; the second sentence does, and it takes *estar*.

A rule of change of state also accounts for why the members of an orchestra *están* in a restaurant, and the instruments *están* already on the stage but the concert *es* in half an hour. In fact, the rule of events taking *ser* makes perfect sense when those events are seen as deletion of the past participle in the passive voice: the concert/the wedding/the talk *es* (PERFORMED) at the chapel at 8:00 PM. Simply put, events are with *ser* because they do not express a change of state. Even when there is a change in venue, *ser* is used: the talk *será* (\**estará*) in Bull Hall, not in Falk Hall, as previously scheduled. An understanding of reporting of events with *ser* as passive voice sentences whose past participle is omitted makes it unnecessary a rule that *ser* is used to express the "location" of events, a rule common in textbooks and in scholarly accounts (e.g. Marín 2016: 22). The current rule of *ser* to express the "location of events" contradicts what we learned about *estar* to express location. However, the specialization of *ser* and *estar* explained in Table 3.2 is consistent with the passive voice (*ser* + past participle) expressing the *occurrence* of an event. People, things, and even abstractions do not occur, but are located: the members of the orchestra *están* in the restaurant, the instruments *están* in the theater, beauty *está* in the eye of the beholder.

*Table 3.2* Red delicious and granny Smith apples in a supermarket

| Red delicious apples in a supermarket | Granny Smith apples in a supermarket |
|---|---|
| • *Están en el supermercado.* 'They are in the supermarket'. | • *Están en el supermercado.* 'They are in the supermarket'. |
| • *Están maduras. (cf. #Son maduras.)*[4] 'They are ripe'. (cf. #They are mature.) | • *Están maduras. (cf. #Son maduras.)* 'They are ripe'. (cf. #They are mature.) |
| • *Son rojas cuando están maduras.* 'They are red when they are ripe'. | • *Son verdes, aunque estén maduras.* 'They are green, even if they are ripe'. |
| • *No están verdes. Están maduras.* 'They are not unripe. They are ripe'. | • *No están verdes. Están maduras, aunque sean de color verde (se vean verdes).* 'They are not unripe. They are ripe, even if their color is green (they look green)'. |
| • *Antes estaban verdes; ahora están rojas.* 'They were green before; now they are red'. | • *Antes eran verdes y siempre serán verdes, aunque estén maduras.* 'They were green (in color) before, and they will always be green (in color), even if they are ripe'. |

At least a dozen "borderline" cases could be addressed here. For example, why is permanent location expressed with *ser* or with *estar*, depending on regional differences? That issue is left to others who can answer some of the questions not addressed here (or that did not occur to us) and who can contribute with more specific suggestions as to how this proposal can begin to be incorporated in textbooks for L2 learners. This chapter is simply taking it up where VanPatten (2010: 35) left off. It is also, of course, an invitation for others to enter the conversation.

In addition to most of the sentences in this chapter, many of which can be easily adapted for presentation in textbooks, even at the elementary level, readers can observe the following list of relatively common participles used as adjectives. When used with *estar*, they invariably express the result of a change; when used with *ser*, they invariably express the passive voice. Students should get a good grasp of what it means to express a change of state if examples with past participles (used as past participles or as adjectives) similar to those below are used. Some explicit attention at the beginning levels might be enough to help students understand an explanation that will reduce the number of rules for *estar* from four to one. The understanding of passive voice and resultant state is worth a few minutes (at different levels, from different angles) of class time, particularly when that explanation can be communicated with well-chosen examples, and without any "linguistese". It is conceivable that a few pairs of images will go a long

*Table 3.3* Past participles commonly used with *estar*, particularly in the present tense

| A few common past participles that favor or require **estar** | | |
|---|---|---|
| *Abierta/o* 'opened' | *Demolida/o* 'demolished' | *Mojada/o* 'wet' |
| *(A)planchada/o* 'ironed' | *Exhausta/o* 'exhausted' | *Maquillada/o* 'wearing makeup' |
| *Arreglada/o* 'dressed up; fixed' | *Imprimida/o (impresa/o)* 'printed' | *Muerta/o* 'dead' |
| *Arrugada/o* 'wrinkled' | *Lavada/o* 'washed' | *Remodelada/o* 'remodeled' |
| *Blanqueada/o* 'bleached' | *Limpiada/o (limpia/o)* 'cleaned/clean' | *Rota/o* 'broken' |
| *Cansada/o* 'tired' | *Llenada/o (llena/o)* 'full' (from *filled*) | *Torcida/o* 'twisted' |
| *Cargada/o* 'loaded' | *Marcada/o* 'marked' | *Vestida/o* 'dressed' |

way in showing clearly change of state vs. the norm and resultant state vs. passive voice in elementary and intermediate textbooks for Spanish. See Table 3.3.

## 3.8. Some implications for teaching

In addition to an answer to VanPatten (2010), this chapter also suggests that the common assumption that the teaching of some grammar in the classroom is not an efficient use of time should be revisited. The teaching of grammar in the classroom is not an efficient use of time because the current grammar in most textbooks is not a learnable theory of the grammar for an L2, as Frantzen (1995; 2013) has shown for preterite and imperfect (many textbook rules are half-truths), as VanPatten (2010) and this chapter suggest for *ser* and *estar*, as Whitley (2002) shows for just about any dichotomy or "hard bone" in Spanish as an L2, and as many others have undoubtedly observed. It is unlikely that native speakers are computing a list of rules (from four to eight or more) for each member of the several dichotomies in Spanish, *ser* and *estar* being just one of them. The rule that *estar* expresses a change of state seems a more plausible and learnable theory for *estar* (and *ser*). The merging of VanPatten (2010) and this proposal leads to the hypothesis that textbooks should start gradually "merging" the rules for *estar* to a single rule of *expressing change of state* and the rules for *ser* to a single rule of *expressing the norm*. The ultimate merge will be one rule of change of state for *estar*. *Ser* is other than a change of state. Or, to state it with eight words instead of eight rules: *estar* expresses change of state; *ser*, the norm.

An issue for further research is how this proposal "transfers" to languages with two copulas. It appears that three of those languages are Catalan, Italian, and Portuguese, just in the Romance languages. This is an invitation to colleagues in those and surely other languages to contribute to this conversation.

## 3.9. Conclusions

A rule that explains more than it was intended for is a rule with predictive power. Change of state is not only the main rule for *estar*; it appears to be the only rule needed for it. Why do speakers of Spanish use *estar* but not *ser* in sentences like the following: *el gato está muerto* 'the cat is dead'; *el gato está afuera* 'outside'; *el gato está vacunado* 'vaccinated'; *el gato está jugando* 'playing'; *el gato está de buen humor* 'the cat is in a good mood'? Why do they use *ser* but not *estar* in sentences like the following: *ese gato es nuestro* 'that cat is ours'; *ese gato es uno de los gaticos de Canela* 'that cat is one of Canela's kittens'; *ese gato es un gato doméstico* 'that cat is a domestic cat'; *ese gato es angora* 'that cat is an Angora cat'; *ese gato es del vecino* 'that cat belongs to the neighbor'? Each of the sentences in the first set of examples expresses a change; none of those in the second set does. As VanPatten (2010) suggested, privileging *estar* might be the way to be more successful in teaching the distinction between *estar* and *ser*. How to do that? Instead of teaching a set of rules for each verb, the focus must be on helping students understand change of state, a more interesting and relevant task. Are native speakers computing the four or so uses of *estar* or are they computing change of state? Acquisitionists and psycholinguists have been asking the first question. The evidence adduced in this chapter suggests that they should be asking the second one. In the meantime, instead of working with itemized rules, textbook writers and teachers ought to begin experimenting with change of state.

Interestingly, change of state is also the main rule for the preterite. With verbs of state (*believe, feel, have, like, own, think*, etc.), the preterite expresses that the participant "*empieza a experimentar el estado o termina de experimentarlo*" 'begins to experience the state or finish experiencing it' (Whitley & González 2016: 164). In other words, the preterite also expresses a change of state. A deep understanding of a resultant state led to the connections explained in this chapter. Indeed, if *estar* is perfective, as many scholars have argued (Bruhn de Garavito 2009; Camacho 2012; Fernández Leborans 1999; Gili Gaya 1985[1961]; King 1992; Luján 1981; Silva-Corvalán 1986; Whitley 2002; among many others), the rule for *estar* and the preterite is deep down the same rule. If *Alicia se preocupó* 'Alice became worried,' then *Alicia está preocupada* 'Alice is worried'; if *Alicia se calmó* 'Alicia calmed down,' then *Alicia está calmada* 'Alice is calm'. Thus, it appears that a theoretical distinction, when well understood and expressed in common terms, can be used in the classroom. Is perfectivity the rule at work? It might be. Whether it is or not, change of state is a rule that L2 learners understand, apply, and retain better than the several rules common in most textbooks. Distinguishing change of state from no change is clearly a more interesting and relevant task for L2 learners, and for sure one worth exploring further in the classroom.

## Notes

1　An IMPLICATURE is anything that is inferred from an UTTERANCE but that is not a condition for the truth of the utterance. (From https://glossary.sil.org/term/implicature)

　　UTTERANCE: An utterance is a natural unit of speech bounded by breaths or pauses.

　　(From: https://glossary.sil.org/term/utterance). (Both last accessed in 2020).

2　Remember that an asterisk (*) before a string of words means that it is ungrammatical or not produced by native speakers.

3　The notation "%"means that the sentence is acceptable to few speakers.

4　The notation "#" means semantically odd or not entailed. (Huddleston & Pullum 2002: 35)

## References

Alonso, Amado & Henríquez Ureña, Pedro. 1941. *Gramática castellana*. Buenos Aires: Losada S.A.

Bruhn de Garavito, Joyce. 2009. Eventive and stative passives: The role of transfer in the acquisition of *ser* and *estar* by German and English L1 speakers. In Collentine, Joseph & García, Maryellen & Lafford, Barbara & Marcos Marín, Francisco (eds.), *Selective proceedings of the 11th hispanic linguistics symposium*, 27–38. Somerville: Cascadilla Proceedings Project. (http://www.lingref.com/document#2200)

Bull, William E. 1942. New principles for some Spanish equivalents of "to be". *Hispania* 25. 433–443. (https://www.jstor.org/stable/334262)

Bull, William E. 1965. *Spanish for teachers: Applied linguistics*. New York: Ronald Press Company.

Camacho, José. 2012. *Ser* and *estar*: The individual/stage-level distinction and aspectual predication. In Hualde, José Ignacio & Olarrea, Antxon & O'Rourke, Erin (eds.), *The handbook of Hispanic linguistics*, 453–476. Malden: Wiley-Blackwell. (https://doi.org/10.1002/9781118228098.ch22)

Carlson, Greg N. 1977. *Reference to kinds in English*. Amherst: University of Massachusetts. (Doctoral dissertation).

Dozier, Eleanor & Iguina, Zulma. 2017. *Manual de gramática. Grammar reference for students of Spanish*, 6th ed. Boston: Cengage Learning. (Instructor's edition).

Falk, Johan. 1979. Ser *y* estar *con atributos adjetivales: Anotaciones sobre el empleo de la cópula en catalán y en castellano*. Uppsala: Acta Universitatis Upsaliensis.

Fernández Leborans, María Jesús. 1999. La predicación: Las oraciones copulativas. In Bosque, Ignacio & Demonte, Violeta (eds.), *Gramática descriptiva de la lengua española*, vol. 2, 2357–2460. Madrid: Espasa.

Franco, Fabiola & Steinmetz, Donald. 1983. *Ser* y *Estar* + adjetivo calificativo en español. *Hispania* 66(2). 176–184. (https://www.jstor.org/stable/341394)

Frantzen, Diana. 1995. Preterite/imperfect half-truths: Problems with Spanish textbook rules for usage. *Hispania* 78. 145–158. (https://www.jstor.org/stable/345237)

Frantzen, Diana. 2013. Using literary texts to reveal problematic rules of usage. *Foreign Language Annals* 46. 628–645. (https://doi.org/10.1111/flan.12057)

Gili Gaya, Samuel. 1985[1961]. *Curso superior de sintaxis española*. 15th reprint. Barcelona: Biblograf.

González, Luis H. 2020. *Cómo entender y cómo enseñar* por *y* para. Londres: Routledge. (https://www.routledge.com/9780367347819)

King, Larry D. 1992. *The semantic structure of Spanish*. Amsterdam: John Benjamins.

Lequerica de la Vega, S. & Salazar, Carmen. 2006. *Avanzando. Gramática española y lectura*, 6th ed. Hoboken: John Wiley & Sons, Inc.

Luján, Marta. 1981. The Spanish copulas as aspectual indicators. *Lingua* 54. 165–210. (DOI:10.1016/0024-3841(81)90068-1)

Marín, Rafael. 2016. Ser y estar. In Gutiérrez-Rexach, Javier (ed.), *Enciclopedia de lingüística hispánica*, vol. 2, 13–24. London: Routledge. (https://www.routledge.com/9781138941380)

Ngram Viewer. 2020. (https://books.google.com/ngrams)

Pastor, Alberto. 2016. Adjetivo. In Gutiérrez-Rexach, Javier (ed.), *Enciclopedia de lingüística hispánica*, vol. 1, 369–379. London: Routledge. (https://www.routledge.com/9781138941380)

RAE (Real Academia Española). 2018. *Diccionario de la Real Academia Española*. (http://dle.rae.es/?id=LxNMdqS) (Last accessed 2020)

SIL International. 2020. (https://glossary.sil.org/term) (Last accessed 2020)

Silva-Corvalán, Carmen. 1986. Bilingualism and language change: The extension of *estar* in Los Angeles Spanish. *Language* 62. 587–608. (http://doi.org/10.1353/lan.1986.0023)

VanPatten, Bill. 1987. Classroom learners' acquisition of *ser* and *estar*: Accounting for developmental patterns. In VanPatten, Bill & Dvorak, Trisha R. & Lee, James F. (eds.), *Foreign language learning*, 19–32. Rowley: Newbery.

VanPatten, Bill. 2010. Some verbs are more perfect than others: Why learners have difficulties with *ser* and *estar* and what it means for instruction. *Hispania* 93(1). 29–38. (http://www.jstor.com/stable/25703391)

Vendler, Zeno. 1957. *Linguistics in Philosophy*. Ithaca: Cornell University Press.

Whitley, M. Stanley. 2002. *Spanish/English contrasts. A course in Spanish linguistics*, 2nd ed. Washington: Georgetown University Press. (http://press.georgetown.edu/book/languages/spanishenglish-contrasts)

Whitley, M. Stanley & González, Luis. 2016. *Gramática para la composición*, 3rd ed. Washington: Georgetown University Press. (http://press.georgetown.edu/book/languages/gramática-para-la-composición-0)

# 4 The preterite is like entering or leaving a room; the imperfect is like staying in it

*Luis H. González and Peter Till*

## 4.1. Introduction

Drawing on the concepts of interval in mathematics, inchoativeness, inceptiveness (Bolinger 1963; Bull 1965), middleness (Whitley 2002), and the work of Guitart (1978), among others, but without invoking these specialized terms, this chapter proposes that the IMPERFECT ASPECT and the PRETERITE ASPECT of the past tense can be explained with two simple rules instead of the six to nine rules in most textbooks for Spanish as a second language (L2). The imperfect expresses that the subject of the sentence is in the middle of an interval; the preterite expresses that the subject enters or leaves an interval. College students understand this rule with the metaphor that the preterite is like entering or leaving a room whereas the imperfect is like staying in the room. The proposed explanation is simpler than scholarly accounts, is easily understood by college students, and explains better several famous or difficult examples in textbooks (i.e. *empezó a llover, *ayer tuve una carta (cf. ayer recibí una carta), tuve/tenía que ir a la biblioteca, siempre supe que ibas a triunfar).*[1]

In a very insightful article, Frantzen (1995) scrutinized the six most common rules for the preterite and the imperfect in 30 Spanish textbooks for L2 learners. She observed that each of those rules is a half-truth: each rule fails to predict accurately whether a native speaker would or would not utter many common sentences. She reformulated five of those rules and added a sixth one. Her rules are better stated and more predictive than the six half-true rules that she wanted to replace, and in Frantzen (2013: 630), she expanded her 1995 rules to include (3) and (4) for the preterite and (5) for the imperfect:

> The preterite is used to signal (1) the beginning of an action/state in the past, (2) the end of an action/state, (3) an action/state in its totality, and (4) a series of actions considered as a whole. The imperfect is used to

signal (1) actions/states in progress at a specific point in the past, (2) habitual past actions, (3) repetitious past actions, (4) planned actions/states in the past, and (5) actions/states projected to the future from a past vantage point, whether planned or not.

Echoing other scholars (e.g. Celce-Murcia 2001; Lunn & Albrecht 1997, among others), Frantzen (2013: 630) reiterated the point that the preterite and the imperfect are better taught using examples from literature because, "Literary contexts improve upon the one-sentence examples that linguists often provide to point out problems with textbook rules, which tend to be sentences out of context created to demonstrate their point succinctly". She adds that examples from literary texts provide a richer context that isolated sentences often lack. A richer context might be needed to better understand the writer's choice of one of the two aspects of the past tense (preterite and imperfect).

As Frantzen (1995: 146) put it, "A good grammar explanation should be unambiguous, reliable, succinct, and easy to remember". Her goal of reducing the six rules to principles inspired us to pursue an explanation with rules that are simpler, easier to apply, and above all, that have more PREDICTIVE POWER than the rules with which scholars, teachers, and students have been working. From the perspective of an L2 learner, a rule has predictive power when that learner can apply that rule to new sentences and correctly determine which of the two aspects should be used, especially in sentences that the learner has never read or heard before.

Drawing on the concept of *interval* in mathematics (explained in §4.3 below), inchoativeness, inceptiveness (beginningness), middleness (Whitley 2002: 117), and mainly on Guitart (1978), this chapter advances an explanation that incorporates the best insights proposed until now by scholars, is stated in terms that are easily understood by students, and is an everyday metaphor.

This proposal is the result of exploring – and abandoning – explanations based on states, activities, accomplishments, and achievements (terms explained below in the section on the imperfect) over a period of five semesters with different students looking at hundreds of sentences from writing by native speakers intended for native speakers. It is unrealistic and ultimately unnecessary to bring those distinctions to the classroom. The metaphor of entering, staying, and leaving a state/action is sufficient, and it seems to capture the native speaker's intuition at work. The observation by several scholars (Guitart 1978; Whitley 2002, Whitley & González 2016, among others) that a handful of verbs do not change meaning in the preterite—contrary to a common rule in textbooks – led to the hypothesis that there has to be a better explanation.

The present proposal is a simplification and reformulation of the notion of state-egressive, state-ingressive, be-ingressive, and persistive predicates; monomial and binomial predicates; and time-partitioning verbs, as proposed in Guitart (1978: 146–149). These distinctions do not belong in the classroom. However, the essence of the intuition behind those notions can be expressed in more accessible terms as *entering a state/action/series of actions or leaving a state/action/series of actions*. The difference between *state* and *action* will be explained below. Figure 4.1 illustrates in the form of a diagram the rule in (1).

(1) The imperfect expresses that the participant was in the middle of a state/action/series of actions. The preterite expresses that the participant entered or left a state/action/series of actions.

## 4.2. The preterite

Let us explain the preterite with the everyday action of entering and leaving a room. If someone crosses the threshold of a door heading inside, then that someone is entering a building or a room. Conversely, if someone crosses the threshold of a door heading outside, that someone is leaving a building or a room. Notice that crossing a door threshold is more often than not a punctual (instant-like) occurrence. That is, entering or leaving a room is a complete action that takes a second (or a fraction of it), and is virtually always complete. The crossing of a door threshold nicely captures the *completeness* and *punctuality* commonly and correctly associated with the preterite. When the preterite refers to a state, entering or leaving it also captures the intuition that the preterite expresses *a change of state* – a third

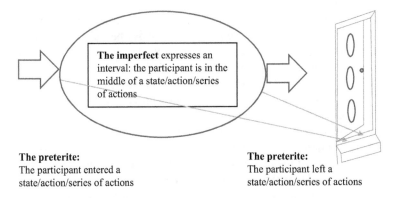

**The imperfect** expresses an interval: the participant is in the middle of a state/action/series of actions

**The preterite:**
The participant entered a state/action/series of actions

**The preterite:**
The participant left a state/action/series of actions

*Figure 4.1* The preterite is like entering or leaving a room; the imperfect is like staying in the room

important property associated with the preterite. The Summer Institute of Linguistics' online Glossary of Linguistic Terms (SIL 2018) offers the following definition:

> A stative verb is a verb that expresses a state of affairs or a state of being rather than an action. Examples: *be, concern, have, know.*

A rule of entering or leaving a state/event/series of events is a better explanation than rules in textbooks. Consider this famous example, easily one of the most common ones in a given number of textbooks, and surely a provocative one. According to many textbooks and scholarly accounts, a rule that the preterite signals "the beginning of an action/state in the past" (Frantzen 2013: 630) explains this example.

(2)   *Empezó a llover*
　　'It began to rain'.

It is uncontroversial that crossing a door threshold captures the main intuition behind the preterite. Crossing a door threshold entails completeness, change of state, and punctuality, all of them properties associated with the preterite. Crossing a door threshold also better explains entering (or leaving!) a state or action. Invoking the beginning of an action/state somehow conjures an image of incompleteness. On the other hand, entering a state does not invite that inference. Likewise, you can leave a state/action, regardless of whether that action is complete. This is consistent with observations by scholars (Bolinger 1963; Guitart 1978; among others) that the preterite is not necessarily terminative. For example, one can say that yesterday one worked (*trabajó*) three hours on a proposal for a talk at a conference, but made little progress.

According to the current understanding of the preterite and the imperfect, the preterite is used in the sentence in (2) above because it expresses the beginning of an action/state in the past. Or the beginning of raining, as stated in just about any textbook. To our knowledge, nobody has observed that *llover* is not in the preterite. It is in the infinitive. The question is whether this sentence (and many similar ones with verbs of *beginning*, and perhaps with other verbs) is expressing beginning. What this sentence is expressing is what the preterite is good at expressing: end. More than the beginning of raining, what the native speaker might be expressing is the opposite: *the end of the beginning.* That is a provocative observation for two reasons. A rule for the preterite that refers to end and to beginning is somewhat suspicious, is it not? Thus, explaining this sentence as the end of the beginning makes more sense, in our opinion. However, our metaphor of entering a room suggests an even better hypothesis: the preterite is there to express entering an action of raining. Is it not true that if we say that *empezó a llover* (it began to rain), we are stating that we entered an action of raining? If that is correct, the prediction of our rule in (1) is that leaving the action of raining should also be expressed with the preterite. That prediction is correct.

(3) Cesó/dejó/paró/terminó de llover.
 'It ceased/stopped/stopped/finished raining'

This section began to show that the preterite aspect of the past tense expresses that a participant in a sentence enters or leaves a state, an action, or a series of actions.

## 4.3. The imperfect

The imperfect expresses that a participant in a sentence is in the middle of an interval, at any point between the start and end of a state/action/series of actions. Petrovic (2018) offers the following definition for *interval*:

> An **interval** is a range of numbers between two given numbers and includes all of the real numbers between those two numbers. As you may recall, **real numbers** are pretty much any number you can think of: 3.56, 171, sqrt 5, –0.157, pi, etc. When the forecaster said that there would be at least 3 but less than 8 inches of snow, he described the amount of snow in an interval! (All emphasis is hers.)

The following is our translation of *intervalo*, as defined by the dictionary of the Royal Academy of the Spanish Language (Real Academia Española 2018):

1. m. Space or distance between one time and another or between one place and another.
2. m. Set of values that take a magnitude between two given limits. *Interval between temperatures, between energies, between frequencies.*
3. m. Mus. Difference in tone between the sound of two musical notes.

As its name suggests, the *imperfect* aspect of the past tense refers to a state/action/series of actions that is seen as *not complete at the time of speaking*. The imperfect makes no reference to the end of a state/action/series of actions even though the state/action/series of actions might have ended. That is the intuition behind the rules for the imperfect, as stated in Frantzen (2013):

The imperfect is used to signal (1) actions/states in progress at a specific point in the past, (2) habitual past actions, (3) repetitious past actions, (4) planned actions/states in the past, and (5) actions/states projected to the future from a past vantage point, whether planned or not.

Vendler (1957) proposed a classification of verbs as states, activities, accomplishments, and achievements, which is widely used in linguistics. Van Valin & Lapolla (1997) give one of the clearest and most complete explanations and applications of these four different classes of verbs to a range of phenomena in several languages belonging to different families. Readers have already seen a definition of state (i.e. stative verbs) from SIL at the beginning of §4.2. Some examples were provided: *be, concern, have, know*. Activities are actions with some duration, but they need not be complete to have occurred (e.g. *run, snore, swim,* etc.). Accomplishments are complete, and they are durative; that is, they are actions that require some time to complete (e.g. *write a speech, memorize a poem, sing a song, watch a movie,* etc.). Achievements are also complete, but they are punctual or instant-like; that is, they are actions that are completed within a second or so of having started (e.g. *pop a balloon, break a vase, see a person* [meaning catch sight of a person], etc.).

This section has briefly explained activities, accomplishments, and achievements, but those distinctions do not belong in the language classroom, obviously. Since states, activities, and accomplishments are durative (they require some time), they lend themselves to be expressed in the imperfect. Achievements are punctual and are often expressed in the preterite. They can, however, be expressed in the imperfect when they are repeated. Breaking a plate is a punctual action. However, if someone used to break a plate every month or so, that action is expressed in Spanish (and presumably in other languages with a similar preterite/imperfect distinction) in the imperfect:

(4)    *Tatiana quebraba un plato cada mes.*
       'Tatiana used to break a plate every month'.

After this brief explanation of actions (activities, accomplishments, achievements), one can go back to the rules for the imperfect and ask, what do the following have in common: in progress (or ongoing, as stated in many textbooks), in the middle, repetitious (the term in Frantzen 1995 for *repeated*), habitual, and planned? They all express states or actions that last for an interval of time (or that imply an ensuing interval in the case of planned actions/states). As just explained, achievements, which are punctual, can be expressed as an interval if the same (or a comparable) achievement happens repeatedly over time, like Tatiana breaking a plate every month. Now state/ action/series of actions can be replaced in the rule in (1) for *interval*, and a rule for the preterite and the imperfect can be stated in as few as 23 words:

(5) The imperfect expresses that the participant was in the middle of an interval.
The preterite expresses that the participant entered it or left it.

Incidentally, it is extremely rare to express age and the time of the day in the past in the preterite. It is straightforward to understand why age is expressed in the imperfect since one has a certain number of years for 365 days at a time, a clear interval. Quite a few events and states obtain during a year for every person. On the other hand, turning X number of years should be in the preterite due to its punctuality, and it is. Although any given time in a day is a point (it was 9:10 PM at the time I was writing this), when time is expressed in the past, it is always in reference to an event (or state) that took place at a point that was in the middle of an interval of time that now stretches to the time of the utterance. Thus, time in the past could refer to a point in an interval that is shorter than 365 days or it can also be a point in an interval that stretches over multiple iterations of 365 days.

## 4.4. Testing this proposal with the famous example *ayer tuve una carta* 'yesterday, I had a letter' and similar examples

Let us consider five related sentences that will show why the rule in (5) is a better explanation for the preterite and the imperfect than current explanations in textbooks and scholarly accounts. Observe the differences in meaning among the sentences in (6a–e). There is no doubt that (6b) means that, for some time, I was in possession of a letter that Shakira had written to me. The crucial question is whether (6c) is quasi-synonymous with (6a), or with (6d), or with (6e).

Note: a translation for sentences (6a–c) is not provided, so readers can try to figure out the meaning on their own. Readers will find an explanation for each sentence in the paragraph following the sentences.

(6) a. *Recibí una carta de Shakira.*
b. *Tenía una carta de Shakira.*
c. *Tuve una carta de Shakira.*
d. *Mi novia me botó/me quemó la carta de Shakira.*
'My girlfriend threw away/burned my letter from Shakira'.

　　e.   *Se me perdió la carta de Shakira.*
　　　　'I lost my letter from Shakira'.

As per the rule in (5), sentence (6a) means that I entered a state of having/
owning a letter from Shakira (i.e. I received a letter from Shakira). (6b)
means that I was in a state of having/owning a letter from Shakira (i.e. I had
– in my possession – a letter that I had previously received from Shakira).
(6c) means that I left the state of having/owning a letter from Shakira (i.e.
I no longer have a letter that I had previously received from Shakira). (6d)
means that I left the state of having/owning a letter from Shakira (because
the letter was thrown away or was burned). (6e) also means that I left a state
of having/owning a letter from Shakira (because I lost the letter).

　　Some might be surprised to read that (6c) means that I left the state of
owning a letter from Shakira. In some textbooks, and in several scholarly
accounts, one can find examples similar to (6c):

(7)   *Ayer tuve una carta de Shakira.*

Does (7) mean that yesterday I got a letter from Shakira? That explanation
is incorrect. A native speaker of Spanish who would like to say that she or
he got a letter from Shakira would say that *recibió una carta de Shakira* 'he/
she received a letter from Shakira', *le llegó una carta de Shakira* 'a letter
from Shakira arrived for her/him' or that *Shakira le escribió* 'Shakira wrote
to her/him'. Notice that each of these three sentences means that the person
entered a state of having/owning a letter from Shakira. Sentence (7) means
that I no longer have a letter that I had received from Shakira. That is, that
sentence means exactly the opposite of what is indicated in many textbooks
and in several scholarly accounts (e.g. Frantzen 1995, 2013; King & Suñer
2007: 88; among others). That example might have been used for the first
time by Bolinger (1963: 130), who wrote, "Yo tenía una carta de ella casi
todos los días 'I had a letter from her almost every day'". It appears that
scholars have not questioned this example from Bolinger, an example that
is incorrect in the imperfect as well. A native would say that he/she *recibía/
le llegaba una carta de ella todos los días*. Interestingly, the problem here
is more the anglicism of imposing on Spanish the English "had/got a letter"
than the aspectual difference.

　　There is substantial evidence for our explanation that (7) means that
the person no longer has the letter, not that the person has just received it.
First, when the authors of this chapter presented this work at a conference
in February 2018, one professor (Kevin Martillo Viner) stated that he was
always suspicious of examples like this one, and that several native speakers had told him that they would never say that they *tuvieron una carta* to

mean that they got a letter; they would say that they *recibieron una carta* 'received a letter' or that *les llegó una carta* 'a letter arrived for them'. Second, consider the following sentences:

(8) a. *Los abuelos tenían una casa en la playa, pero la vendieron.*
'My grandparents used to have a beach house, but they sold it'.
 b. *Los abuelos tuvieron una casa en la playa. #Este fin de semana vamos para allá.*
'My grandparents had a beach house. #This weekend, we are going there'.
 c. *Los abuelos tenían/tuvieron una casa en la playa. Echamos de menos las vacaciones que solíamos pasar allá.*
'My grandparents used to have/had a beach house. We miss the vacations that we used to spend there'.

(The notation '#' before a sentence means that the sentence is not entailed by the sentence in question – the sentence before it, in this case. Sentence X entails sentence Y if every time X is true, Y is true. Both the notation and this definition of entailment come from Huddleston & Pullum 2002: 35).

Sentence (8a) means that my grandparents used to have a beach house for some time. "But they sold it" confirms that they no longer have it. Note that the imperfect does not tell us whether my grandparents still have the beach house or not. Only when *la vendieron* 'they sold it' is given, do we know that they no longer have the house. Sentence (8b) means that my grandparents no longer have a house at the beach; not that they recently received a house. Therefore, we cannot go to that house this weekend. Sentence (8c) also means that they no longer have the house, as the second sentence in (8c) makes it clear. The clue in the second sentence in (8c) is so clear, that the imperfect is not only possible; it is the most common way of expressing this state of affairs. Indeed, as many scholars have observed (Gili Gaya 1985[1961]; Guitart 1978; Whitley 2002; among others), the imperfect expresses an action in the middle (an interval in our terms), and then the speaker proceeds to add something else that happened, often in the preterite.

Let us now add to the two previous pieces of evidence, three more pieces from literary sources to the interpretation proposed for (7).

First, there is a verse from a song that makes reference to age with *tener* 'have' in the preterite, an extremely uncommon occurrence, compared with *tener* in the imperfect to express age in the past. (A Google search in May 2018 for "*yo tenía veinte años*" returned 24,700 hits; "*yo tuve veinte años*" returned 423 hits).

(9)   *Yo también tuve veinte años y un corazón vagabundo,*
      *yo también tuve alegrías y profundos desengaños.*
      'I was also twenty years old and I had a vagabond heart,
      I had happy days as well as deep disappointments'. (Morales 2020)

The meaning of (9) is, of course, that I am no longer 20 years old; not that I turned 20.

Second, as Guitart (1978: 144) observed, the following two sentences "are roughly equivalent" (his sentences 29a and 29b):

(10) a.   *Él tenía dinero y ya no tiene.*
          'He had money and now he doesn't'. (Guitart's gloss)
     b.   *Él tuvo dinero.*
          'He had money'. (Guitart's gloss)

As Guitart himself observes, "The fact that a stative predicate in the PRET[erite] tells that the state is no longer in effect does not mean that PRET[erite] is basically terminative". Sentence (10b) means that he had money and now he does not, not that he has just gotten some money.

Third, consider these verses from Poema XX by Pablo Neruda:

(11) (The number preceding each line is the verse number in the poem)
     6 Yo la quise, y a veces ella también me quiso.
     7 En las noches como esta la tuve entre mis brazos.
     8 La besé tantas veces bajo el cielo infinito.
     9 Ella me quiso, a veces yo también la quería.
     23 Ya no la quiero, es cierto, pero cuánto la quise.
     24 Mi voz buscaba el viento para tocar su oído.
     29 Porque en noches como esta la tuve entre mis brazos,

Eight out of ten verbs in the past tense are forms of *tener* or *querer*. Seven out of those eight are in the preterite, and they clearly express that the participant left that state, not that the participant entered it.

Let us summarize our explanation of the sentences in (6) as in (12), using the explanation proposed in Figure 4.1:

(12) a.   *Recibí una carta de Shakira.* = I entered a state of owning a letter
          from Shakira.
     b.   *Tenía una carta de Shakira.* = I was in the state of owning a letter
          from Shakira.

c. *Tuve una carta de Shakira.* = I left the state of owning a letter from Shakira.

d. *Mi novia me botó/quemó la carta de Shakira.* = Same as (12c)

e. *Se me perdió la carta de Shakira.* = Same as (12c)

If there is still any doubt, the reader should consider (13):

(13) *En el 2007 estuve en México, DF.*
'In 2007, I was in Mexico, DF'.

The sentence in (13) means that I went to México, DF, in 2007, but that I am no longer in México. How, then, do I express the fact that I arrived in México, DF, on August 7, 2007? I would say that I arrived in Mexico that day: *Llegué a México el día 7 de agosto del 2007* 'I arrived in Mexico on August 7, 2007'. An attentive reader might ask how to account for sentences similar to (14a) and (14b).

(14) a. *Estuve en el aeropuerto a la 1:30 para recogerte.*
'I was at/arrived at/got to the airport at 1:30 to pick you up'.

b. *Te estuve esperando hasta que anunciaron que el vuelo había sido desviado a Cancún.*
'I was waiting for you until they announced that your flight had been diverted to Cancun'.

c. *Ya estaba en la casa descansando cuando me llamaste diciendo que el vuelo había sido cambiado de nuevo.*
'I was already relaxing at home when you called me saying that the flight had been changed back again'.

Sentence (14a) seems to contradict our explanation. It does not. It means that I entered the state of being at the airport at 1:30. (14b) means that I left the state of waiting for you at the airport. *Anunciaron* means that I entered the state of knowing that information. (14c) means that I was in a state of relaxing at home when you *llamaste*, which means I entered the state of knowing a different piece of information.

Finally, some readers might be wondering how to account for the past perfect (the *pluscuamperfect*) used in *había sido desviado* and *había sido cambiado*. The intuition behind the past perfect is that it expresses an action/state further in the past than another action/state; hence one of its names, pluscuamperfect, 'more (past) than another past tense'. In order to avoid a longer tangent, it suffices to say that the preterite perfect (*hubo desviado, hubo sido desviado*) is a dead tense in Spanish, presumably because its meaning was so close to the simple preterite that any difference in meaning was negligible. As a result, the imperfect of *haber* is virtually the choice by default to form a past perfect (in the indicative) in Spanish. Whitley & González (2016: 222) offer an explanation that teachers and students can easily understand, including the past perfect in indirect discourse. Incidentally, the past perfect (*ella había llamado* 'she had called') and the present perfect (*ha llamado* 'she has called') are names adapted from English in the teaching of Spanish as an L2 because those names are very intuitive; more so than the names in Spanish.

### 4.5. Testing this proposal with examples from five different textbooks for beginning to advanced levels

The reader is invited to confirm how enter/leave a state/action/series of actions explains all of the examples with the preterite on the left. Likewise, being in the middle of an interval explains all of the examples on the right column. These are all examples from five different textbooks for beginning to advanced levels. See Table 4.1

*Table 4.1* All of these examples come from the explanation for preterite/imperfect in five different textbooks for beginning to advanced levels

| *Preterite: the participant ENTERED OR LEFT a state/action/series of actions* | *Imperfect: the participant was IN THE MIDDLE of a state/action/series of actions* |
| --- | --- |
| Ayer recibí seis llamadas telefónicas. | Mi marido siempre me llamaba a las cuatro de la tarde. |
| Mi amigo Antonio no anunció su visita. | Antonio nunca anunciaba sus visitas. |
| Antonio vino a Estados Unidos … | … cuando tenía cinco años. |
| Llegamos en avión, recogimos las maletas y fuimos al hotel. | Era un día oscuro. Llovía de vez en cuando. |
| Empezó a llover más fuerte. | Llovía sin parar. |
| La familia de Botero se sorprendió … | … porque cuando era pequeño, él quería ser torero. |
| Ayer me lavé el pelo. | Lo tenía muy sucio. |
| También me corté el pelo. | Mi pelo estaba muy largo. |
| Anoche fuimos al cine. | Íbamos a ir al teatro caminando. |
| Pero decidimos ir en carro. | Parecía que iba a llover. |
| Vimos una casa que nos gustó mucho. El banco nos aprobó un préstamo. | Buscábamos una casa porque mi mamá y mi papá ya esperaban el tercer hijo. |
| Un día, el tío Guillermo preparó una sopa de pescado. La probé y me gustó mucho. | Antes de ese día, no me gustaba el pescado. |

Observe that background or description is an interval. Therefore, if we have a rule of interval, there is no need for a rule that the imperfect is used to describe in the past (as opposed to narrate). Background information or description is in the imperfect because the speaker/writer is taking the listener/reader to the middle of an interval. Only when an entering or leaving happens does the speaker/writer move the narration with the preterite.

Table 4.2 presents in two columns a short exercise to discuss how when the imperfect is used, the speaker/reader is expressing that the participant is in the middle of an interval; when the preterite is used, the participant enters or leaves a state/event/series of events.

This section has taken examples from five different textbooks. We were able to explain all of them with our rule in (5). A short reading passage that can be used to explain our rule of being in the interval or entering/leaving it was used. Both exercises can be adapted to the level being taught or to the level of any particular class.

*Table 4.2* A short exercise showing examples for preterite/imperfect

| *Preterite: the participant ENTERED OR LEFT a state/action/series of actions* | *Imperfect: the participant was in the middle of a state/action/series of actions* |
|---|---|
| | Ayer tenía que estudiar para un examen de cálculo. El problema es que el equipo de la U tenía un partido de basquetbol muy importante. |
| | ¿Iba al partido o estudiaba? |
| Decidí que … | … podía ir al partido o estudiar. |
| | Si estudiaba y no miraba las noticias, podía ver el partido después del examen. |
| Hice eso: estudié para el examen y lo presenté. | |
| Después de tomar el examen, miré el video del partido sin leer sobre él. Tengo que admitir que no fue realmente igual. Lo bueno fue que saqué la mejor calificación en el examen. ¡Mi plan funcionó! | ¡No lo podía creer! |

## 4.6. Verbs do *not* change meaning when used in the preterite

Verbs like *conocer, costar, poder, querer, saber, tener* (like any other verb) express that the participant is in the middle of an interval when used in the imperfect; if the participant enters or leaves that interval, that state/event is expressed in the preterite. When an interval is seen in its entirety, the preterite is called for. Remember that SIL defines a state as, "A stative verb is a verb that expresses a state of affairs or a state of being rather than an action". Their examples were verbs like *be, concern, have,* and *know.*

Due to the fact that these authors arrived at the rule for entering or leaving a state/action/series of actions while trying to understand literally dozens of examples of the so-called "meaning-changing preterites", we now turn to all of the examples discussed by Frantzen (2013) in the section on "meaning-changing preterites" (her examples 14 to 23, each example being a short paragraph or two, with typically at least three such verbs). This time, the authors will simply copy and comment on the sentences having one of these verbs. (Following Frantzen 2013, each preterite or imperfect discussed is in bold type for convenience.) Frantzen (2013: 634) observes that many scholars have cautioned against the meaning-change explanation. Frantzen uses (some of) her new nine rules.

The following examples come from Frantzen (2013: 634–636):

1. *De niña nadie la **conoció***: Nobody entered the state of knowing her. If nobody entered the state of knowing her, the prediction is that *nadie la conocía* (nobody knew her). This implicature is valid because the girl moved to the town with her Mom when the girl was already a woman.
2. *Limpio de cuerpo y alma como yo te **conocí***: The female character entered the state of knowing him, and the *conocer* is portrayed in its entirety. Interestingly, the character is not dead, but his companion is wishing him to find a woman who can make him happy.
3. *Después **supe** mejor, la contracción de las branquias, el tanteo de las finas patas* […]: Entered the state of knowing.
4. *Lo **supe** antes de esto, antes de ser un axolotl*: Entered the state of knowing.
5. *Lo **supe** el día en que me acerqué a ellos por primera vez*: Entered the state of knowing.
6. *Con un chorro de palabras inventadas que **tuvieron** la virtud de espantarle el deseo.* Those words had the virtue of forcing the character into

a state of scaring away his desire. If the reader thinks about the difference between *tenía que ir a la tienda* 'I had to go to the store' (i.e. was supposed to go) and *tuve que ir a la tienda* 'I was supposed to go the store, and I went', then *tuvieron* clearly means that the words had the expected result, the meaning intended. *Tenían* would mean that the words had the potential, but we do not know whether that potential ended up in a result.

7.  *Edu **tenía** entonces veinticuatro años y aquel era su primer papel importante*: Age and time are expressed overwhelmingly in the imperfect. Sometime during the interval of a year, he was given that role in *Bodas de sangre*.

8.  *Era un poco joven para el papel y, además, José Luis decía que no daba el tipo, **quería** a alguien más agresivo y agitado* [...]: For some time, José Luis was in the middle of his wanting a different actor.

9.  *José Luis transigió por complacerme, pero le **tuvo** siempre un poco enfilado*: The adverb *siempre* and the *preterite* of *tener* express the entirety of a state/action, as observed by Frantzen (2013: 635). In our terms, it refers to the entirety of the interval (perhaps more precisely to its end), not to its middle.

10. *Ella **quiso** saber la causa de tanto maltrato*: She entered the state of wanting, and that wanting was "executed". As Frantzen explains, the author might have used *asked*. *Quiso* means that the wanting was not in the middle; it was satisfied. The implicature is that she inquired, and she received an answer. If this explanation is somewhat difficult to grasp, it is perhaps because if a speaker wanted to do something and did it, there is not much of a point in expressing the wanting; the speaker can just simply state what they did. On the other hand, *no quiso saber* (she did not want to know) would be not entering the state of knowing. The exploration of the frequency of *quiso* vs. *no quiso* is left for future research. The prediction is that the latter should be more frequent. For example, *no quería ir al partido, pero sus amigas la convencieron* 'she did not want [imperfect] to go to the game, but her friends convinced [preterite] her'. *No quiso ir al partido y no fue* 'she did not want [preterite] to go to the game, and she did not go'. The latter sentence can simply be stated as *no fue al partido* 'she did not go to the game'. Or *no fue al partido porque no quería* 'she did not go [preterite] to the game because she did not want to [imperfect]'; *no fue al partido porque no podía* 'she did not go [preterite] to the game because she could [imperfect] not go'.

11.  *La respuesta dejó atónita a la muchacha, pero **no quiso** parecer descarada y se limitó* […]: She did not enter the state of being regarded as shameless.

12.  —*No **quise** decir eso, reina*: The character did not want to enter the action of saying what he said, but apparently, he did.

Note: We had written our prediction about *no quiso* being perhaps more frequent than *quiso*. We assure the reader that we had not noticed the last two examples. Thus, we have one sentence with *quiso* and two with *no quiso*.

After having explained all of the twelve examples from Frantzen (2013) referring to this rule ("meaning-changing preterites"), the discussion proceeds with two examples that help students in understanding the aspectual difference. Referring to the first one, a college student (Allie Blum) said in class in 2015, "I have never seen the contrast between the preterite and the imperfect so clearly before". The reader can try to see the difference before reading the explanation after the examples.

(15)  a.  *Esta mañana no quise* [preterite] *afeitarme.*
'This morning, I did not want to shave'.
    b.  *Esta mañana no quería* [imperfect] *afeitarme.*
'This morning, I did not want to shave'.

With one of the sentences, the reader knows for sure that the speaker did not shave. With the other sentence, the reader does not know for sure: the speaker could have shaved, or could have not. The first scenario corresponds to the preterite in (15a); the second, to the imperfect in (15b).

Finally, the prediction is that if the authors really mean to finish, then they should say – and mean it – that this section finally ended. Would native speakers say that the section *terminaba* [imperfect] or *terminó* [preterite]? The latter, of course.

## 4.7.  Some implications for teaching

Let us do the implications with a question that two different teachers have asked at two different conferences where parts of this chapter were presented. Can teachers use the explanation proposed in this chapter in the classroom? The answer is yes. This author has been fine-tuning and using it for several years. It might look a little more difficult than what we currently do because it is new; not because it is more difficult. It takes some time to adjust to new ways of doing things. This author would like to share what an undergraduate student wrote after he read this chapter. He was in a Spanish advanced grammar and writing class during his second semester in college.

I sent a couple of chapters to him and wanted a general impression of readability. This is one of the several paragraphs he wrote about this chapter. Observe that he uses "tenses". I did not edit his answer at all:

I believe the chapter is so effective for a few reasons. For one, the two main concepts of changing a state of being, and of an interval, are both readily understood and easily grasped by the reader. Secondly, the explanation of how these concepts can be applied to grammar is phenomenal. You take the two well-known concepts of change in state and of intervals and demonstrate how to think about them in the setting of a conversation. Although the reader has probably never thought of their conversation topics in terms of intervals or states of being, it is an easily understood process and quickly feels natural. And finally, the examples are where everything falls into place. The examples are, to me, the most powerful teachers in the whole chapter. They force the reader to work through a problem on their own and apply what they have just read. The explanations following the examples then provide a step-by-step understanding of which tense is correct/incorrect and why. At no point does the reader get left behind – that is, if they do not get the example questions right, they are not left to figure out the reasoning on their own; instead, the reader receives a complete guide as to why one tense is the better choice over the other. From the examples and explanations, the reader gains a full understanding of how to approach a preterite vs. imperfect question.

As for how to present this explanation in the classroom, examples similar to those in the following table can supplement Figure 4.1. The examples can be adapted to different levels. Illustrations and perhaps video clips can enhance presentation. After the 2020 lockdown, one can imagine that visual support will receive a lot more attention now that we know that distant learning might be a reality or at least an option that we might have to get used to. See Table 4.3.

## 4.8. Conclusions

The preterite is very similar to entering a room or leaving it. Therefore, it is complete, entails change, and it tends to be punctual (instant-like). The imperfect is very similar to staying in a room, a situation that is open-ended, durative, and unchanged. Descriptions are often in the imperfect because a given scene, scenario, or stage has these three properties, not because there is a rule that descriptions are in the imperfect. That rule was never invoked in this explanation. If there is a change in that room (or stage, scene, or scenario), our explanation predicts that such a change will be expressed in the preterite. That prediction is correct. A change of state is indeed a more

104   *The preterite and the imperfect*

*Table 4.3* A possible template to illustrate the rule in (1)/Figure 4.1

| Preterite: the participant entered a state/action/series of actions | Imperfect: the participant was in the middle of a state/action/series of actions | Preterite: the participant left a state/action/series of actions |
| --- | --- | --- |
| Empezó a llover a las 8:00. 'It began to rain at 8:00'. | A las 12:00 todavía llovía. 'At 12:00 it was still raining'. | Paró de llover a la 1:00. 'It stopped raining at 1:00'. |
| Hoy no quise afeitarme. (Implies that I did not shave) 'I did not want to shave today, and I did not'. | Hoy no quería afeitarme, pero mi esposa me dijo que no podía ir al trabajo con barba. 'I did not want to shave today, but my wife told me that I could not go to work with a beard'. | Me afeité porque le hice caso a mi esposa. 'I paid attention to my wife, and I shaved'. |
| Recibí una carta de Shakira. 'I received a letter from Shakira'. | Tenía cartas de Shakira y de Natalia Lafourcade. 'I used to have letters from Shakira and from Natalia Lafourcade'. | Mi esposa me botó las cartas de otras amigas. 'My wife threw away my letters from other friends'. |
| Ayer supe que venías hoy. 'I found out/ learned yesterday that you were coming today'. | No sabía que venías con tu esposa. 'I did not know that you were coming with your wife'. | Se me olvidó que me advertiste (me habías advertido). 'I forgot that you warned me (you had warned me)'. |
| El Presidente empezó el discurso a tiempo. 'The President began his speech on time'. | Hablaba cuando hubo un temblor de tierra. 'He was talking when there was an earthquake'. | Paró de hablar y todo el mundo salió del edificio. 'He stopped speaking and everyone left the building'. |
| Mis padres compraron una casa en la playa. 'My parents bought a house at the beach'. | La casa era de los abuelos. (La casa les pertenecía a los abuelos). 'The house used to belong to our grandparents'. | Los abuelos la vendieron porque se cansaron de recibir visitas sin anunciar. 'Our grandparents sold it because they got tired of receiving unannounced visits'. |

accurate way of expressing the intuition that the preterite "advances" the narration, a rule in some textbooks that these authors have some respect for. One of the authors remembers Dr. Bill Maisch at The University of North Carolina at Chapel Hill highlighting this rule.

Reading a book is an accomplishment that can take hours over a period of days, weeks, and even months. When is the reading of a book expressed with the preterite because it is viewed as point-like, as crossing that door threshold? When one reads the last word, in the last paragraph, on the last page of the last chapter. Only then can one say that *leyó* [preterite] *el libro* 'read the book'. At that moment, the reading of a book – an accomplishment due to its duration – can be expressed as an achievement: the reader has *instantly* entered the state of having read the whole book. You, dear reader, have achieved that accomplishment if you have read just about every word in this book and this last word.

## Note

1   Remember that an asterisk (*) before a string of words means ungrammatical or not produced by native speakers.

## References

Bolinger, Dwight L. 1963. Reference and inference: Inceptiveness in the Spanish preterit. *Hispania* 46. 128–135. (https://www.jstor.org/stable/336957)

Bull, Wiliam E. 1965. *Spanish for teachers. Applied linguistics.* New York: Ronald Press Company.

Celce-Murcia, Mariane. 2001. Why it makes sense to teach grammar in context and through discourse. In Hinkel, Eli & Fotos, Sandra (eds.), *New perspectives on grammar teaching in second language classrooms*, 119–133. London: Routledge.

Frantzen, Diana. 1995. Preterite/imperfect half-truths: Problems with Spanish textbook rules for usage. *Hispania* 78. 145–158. (https://www.jstor.org/stable/345237)

Frantzen, Diana. 2013. Using literary texts to reveal problematic rules of usage. *Foreign Language Annals* 46. 628–645. (https://doi.org/10.1111/flan.12057)

Gili Gaya, Samuel. 1985[1961]. *Curso superior de sintaxis española.* 15th reprint. Barcelona: Biblograf.

Guitart, Jorge. 1978. Aspects of Spanish aspect: A new look at the preterit/imperfect distinction. *Contemporary studies in Romance linguistics* 5. 132–168.

Huddleston, Rodney & Pullum, Geoffrey K. 2002. *The Cambridge grammar of the English language.* Cambridge: Cambridge University Press.

Kind, Larry D. & Suñer, Margarita. 2007. *Gramática española: Análisis y práctica.* Boston: McGraw-Hill Education.

Lunn, Patricia V. & Albrecht, Jane. 1997. The grammar of technique: Inside "Continuidad de los parques". *Hispania* 80. 227–233. (https://www.jstor.org/stable/345881)

Morales, José A. 2020. Yo también tuve 20 años. Song. (https://www.youtube.com/watch?v=Yul0ogWdy6c) (Last accessed 2020)

Ngram Viewer. 2020. (https://books.google.com/ngrams)

Petrovic, Allison. 2018. What is an interval in math? (https://study.com/academy/lesson/what-is-an-interval-in-math.html) (Last accessed 2020)

RAE (Real Academia Española). 2020. Diccionario de la Real Academia Española. (http://dle.rae.es/?id=LxNMdqS) (Last accessed 2020)

SIL (The Summer Institute of Linguistics). 2018. *Glossary of linguistic terms.* (https://glossary.sil.org/term/stative-verb) (Last accessed 2020)

Van Valin, Robert D. & LaPolla, Randy J. 1997. *Syntax: Structure, meaning, and function.* Cambridge: Cambridge University Press.

Vendler, Zeno. 1957. *Linguistics in philosophy.* Ithaca: Cornell University Press.

Whitley, M. Stanley. 2002. *Spanish/English contrasts. A course in Spanish linguistics*, 2nd ed. Washington: Georgetown University Press. (http://press.ge orgetown.edu/book/languages/spanishenglish-contrasts)

Whitley, M. Stanley & González, Luis. 2016. *Gramática para la composición*, 3rd ed. Washington: Georgetown University Press. (http://press.georgetown.edu/bo ok/languages/gramática-para-la-composición-0)

# Index